THE HUMAN ADVENTURE

THE HUMAN ADVENTURE

THE ART OF
CONTEMPLATIVE LIVING

William McNamara, OCD

AMITY HOUSE
Amity, New York

Grateful acknowledgment is made to the following for permission to use previously published material:

Excerpt from "Little Gidding," part of *Four Quartets* by T. S. Eliot. Reprinted by permission of Harcourt, Brace Jovanovich, Inc.

Extracts from *Christian Zen* by William Johnston, copyright © 1971 by William Johnston. Reprinted by permission of Harper & Row, Publishers.

Excerpt from "Directive" from *The Poetry of Robert Frost* edited by Edward Connery Lathem, copyright © 1947, 1969 by Holt, Rinehart and Winston, Inc. Reprinted by permission of the publisher.

From "A Woman Wrapped in Silence," copyright © 1941, 1969 by John W. Lynch. Reprinted by permission of Macmillan Publishing Co., Inc.

"A Sleep of Prisoners" by Christopher Fry, copyright 1951 by Christopher Fry. Reprinted by permission of Oxford University Press, Inc.

Excerpt from "God's Grandeur" by Gerard Manley Hopkins by courtesy of Oxford University Press, Inc.

Extract from *A Thousand Clowns* by Herb Gardner, copyright © 1961, 1962 by Herb Gardner and Irvin A. Cantor, Trustee. Reprinted by permission of Random House, Inc.

From *Decline of Pleasure* by Walter Kerr, copyright © 1962 by Walter Kerr. Reprinted by permission of Simon and Schuster, Inc.

Published by Amity House Inc.
16 High Street
Warwick, NY 10990

Copyright © 1974 by William McNamara

Library of Congress Catalog Card Number 87-72988

ISBN 0-916349-28-4

Contents

To the Nada and Nova Nada community and to Shana, Fauna, Siva, Yin and Yang, Tarsus and Allah, whom God loved and man destroyed

Preface

Every time a man goes out among men he returns home less a man. That morbid statement comes from a classic piece of religious literature. It always made me think of the author of *The Imitation of Christ* as a priggish and prudish chap. But it occurs to me now that I might have been outrageously wrong.

I just returned to my hermitage in the woods of Nova Scotia after a two-month "road trip." During that time I crossed the United States twice, lecturing and conducting retreats. I will not leave these woods again for six months. Even then I will not be anxious to depart. Right now I am uproariously happy to be home. This recent trip drained me. I feel like Thomas a Kempis: less a man. But the reasons for my human impoverishment may be different from his. I don't know. I do know, however, that it is extremely difficult to improve your human condition and the human quality of your life in a dehumanized world.

My grievance with contemporary society is with its decrepitude. There are few towering pleasures to allure me, almost no beauty to bewitch me, nothing erotic to arouse me, no intellectual circles or positions to challenge or provoke me, no burgeoning philosophies or theologies and no new art to catch my attention or engage my mind, no rousing political, social, or religious movements to stimulate or excite me. There are no free men to lead me. No saints to inspire me. No sinners sinful enough to either impress me or share my plight. No one human enough to validate the "going" life-style. It is hard to linger in that dull world without being dulled.

People ask me: "How do you justify your solitary life?" I should be asking them: "How do you justify the rat race? How can you abdicate your responsibility to become human, to become more gracefully and creatively involved, as free men—thoughtful, leisurely lovers—in the human adventure? How can you refuse to live fully wherever you are, when that is the whole purpose of being a Christian?"

This book is an attempt to explore some of the dimensions of this subject. The reader may choose to think there are many contradictions in these pages. I have been inclined to think so myself, but have chosen to regard the apparent contradictions as paradoxes. The levels of the human adventure, the Christian exploration into God, examined in this book are necessarily paradoxical. Only the mystic ventures far enough to leave perplexing polarities behind and reconcile opposites. At that point it may even be difficult to tell who is God and who is man.

Writing this book in the woods with no electricity and hardly a library was a challenge. The challenge was met stoutheartedly by our whole community of hermits. My eight cohorts prodded and encouraged me from beginning to end; then, in a great deadline fury, they typed, read, and corrected the manuscript. How impressively they confirmed a basic contention of mine: Solitaries make the best community!

One final thought: This is a serious book; but I hope the reader will not take either me or the book too seriously. A person immersed in the human adventure takes God so seriously that he reads books lightheartedly. If no one leaps from these cool, abstract pages into a living experience, into the consuming fire of God's love, I shall regret this book.

And a prayer:

Divinely empower us, O Lord, to take hold of the brightness of this tiny world, and to defend and protect it against the gray-minded, penny-souled upstarts whose sole ambition is to extinguish your fire and geld humanity of its laughter.

HUMAN EXPERIENCE

Chapter 1 – The Art of Contemplation

Contemplation is the central human act that puts us perceptively and lovingly in touch with the innermost reality of everything because it is a simple intuition of the truth.

I think I can trace most, if not all, of the evils of our day to superficiality on all levels of existence; and this vapidity is due to the absence of contemplation. Man fell when he fell from contemplation. The inevitable consequence was the dehumanization of his individual condition and his social history. We are now reaping the barren results of that bad seed. And so, E. I. Watkin, probably the greatest living philosopher in the world today, claims as the most pressing need of the day the reaffirmation of the metaphysical order of being. And it is by contemplation, and contemplation alone, he says, that the order of being is apprehended.

If contemplation puts us *in touch with the real*, then, above all other things, we ought to become contemplatives, because we are a lonely crowd of alienated people. If it empowers us—perhaps it is better to say humbles and sensitizes us—to penetrate the inner *suchness* of things, then our primary obligation is to become contemplative, because we are hollow men who live halfheartedly on the surface of life: a merely derivative existence.

I insist, as the Gospels do, on metaphysical intuition as the first important phase of the human adventure. Those who skip it and come along for the ride miss one entire dimension of the humanness that makes the adventure worthwhile. Such drifters, floaters, playboys, remain deprived human beings from beginning to end, are a burden to the community and a source of amusement to the world. The metaphysical intuition needed for human adventuring is often a fruit of self-education rather than schooling, of common sense rather than scholarship. I do not mean a timeless metaphysics, but a temporalistic doctrine of being, the radical consequences of a doctrine of love. In our age love has become a bromide. Divorced from objective knowledge, it has become banalized and reduced to sheer sentimentality. Love of the other involves a careful knowledge of the structures of the beloved's world; the structures of human existence, and their discernment, require impartial, loving judgment, united with critical reflection. Our vocation is to love. But love must be rooted in truth.

That is why we need metaphysics that is not a search for being beyond all existence and experience. It is not a speculation about remote causes. It is a simple, intuitive grasp of those general ideas that are necessary for the description of every aspect of experience.

So my first broad recommendation for developing the art of contemplation, in general, is this: an honest-to-goodness, down-to-earth intellectual life. And toward this end I would suggest a re-reading of *The Art of Thinking,* by Ernest Dimnet; *How to Read a Book,* by Mortimer Adler; *Degrees of Knowledge,* by Jacques Maritain; *Insight,* by Bernard Lonergan; *House of Intellect,* by Jacques Barzun; and *The Intellectual Life,* by A. Sertillanges. Along with this first recommendation, however, comes a warning: Do not overdo it; do not get stuck there. It's just a step, though an unskippable one in the art of contemplating. The contemplative life is far more than the intellectual life. It's the intellectual life broadened, widened, deepened, and magnificently simplified. It's our "everyday mind" exploring the "inscape" of things, their implications and connections; making dangerous, dreadful, and delightful forays into the unmapped areas of the self—that is, the subliminal mind—and through this deep center of the soul into the "placiest" place of all, where all men are at home: God, the uncreated and inexhaustible ground of our being.

The contemplative and adventurous exploration into God requires an exquisitely balanced and wholly developed human instrument. We must make the whole psychophysical organism do as many things as possible in order to perfect the whole mind and thus become capable of an intellectual act of the love of God. Such is the educative process that leads to contemplation. Here there is no pedantic intellectualism, no preoccupation with states of consciousness, and no paltry, pietistic love divorced from insight and the pain of responsibility. Instead you have a whole man, activating all of his human potentialities, learning to be a multiple amphibian, at home in many worlds—a noble, classical man because of his *loving awareness of God*.

Here is a good criterion for the kind of intellectual life genuine contemplation requires: You can cultivate the intellectual life for all it is worth only if the love it generates becomes more important than the problems you are trying to solve or dissolve. Academic disciplines are appropriate means to the extent that they habituate you to *wisdom:* literally, a taste for the right things; ultimately, a taste for God. When that divine taste rules you and orders your existence, you are contemplative, whether you are in college, in a monastery, in the marketplace, or in the suburbs.

The intellectual life is the first step toward contemplation. As a mental discipline it empowers man to gather all worthwhile things into focus and to eliminate what is trivial, irrelevant, or merely sentimental. It is imperative to take these first deliberately thoughtful steps and not try to leap instantaneously into states of mind that superficially resemble contemplation.

This saltatory acquisition of an ersatz contemplation is less common among Catholics due to the balanced structure of a sacramental humanism. However, in neo-Catholic Pentecostalism, a charismatic movement within the Church, this tendency toward instant everything is dominant. Consequently, spurious prayer forms often take the place of genuine communion with God, and contrived pseudoexperiences just as frequently preclude the Christian experience of God. The drive toward instant everything—success, power, freedom, intimacy, mysticism—seems, at this point in history, both universal and irresistible.

Most of us, however, are drawn into the opposite kind of trap.

Instead of skipping steps, we multiply them and repeat them end-
lessly—a perpetual roundelay of words, signs, symbols, rules, laws,
ritual, work—and so we fragment and exhaust ourselves in monumental trivia; we thwart and frustrate our towering human purposes by formalism and legalism. We tend to become dilettantes:
more in love with the way than with the end; or psychidolaters:
so fascinated by the inner workings of the psyche that we never
break through and beyond to the eternal and the infinite; or fanatics who, forgetting or afraid of the end, multiply the means.

I have a favorite example of such fanaticism. One day when I
was sitting alone in Austin and Rita Crawford's house in Providence, Rhode Island, my hometown, three Jehovah's Witnesses
came in to convert me. There was a middle-aged woman, a young
boy, and an exquisitely beautiful girl about nineteen years of age.
I was immediately struck by her extraordinarily splendid face and
graceful body. To my delight she turned out to be the speaker.
So on and on she went, reading the Bible sonorously and com-
menting on the inspired passages superbly. There was nothing I
could object to. So after a long period of enraptured listening, I
broke in and said clearly and unequivocally, "I believe." But the
charming lector went on and on, undisturbed by the fact that her
mission was accomplished: I believed. I figured she was a fanatic.
So I ceased to listen and just contemplated her glorious body. The
next time she stopped to take a breath, I exclaimed, "Gosh, you're
beautiful!" Stunned and chagrined, the three abruptly left the
house. They wanted to work on me, not share a common faith
and evoke love. They were dedicated to means, not ends. Here
they had achieved two great ends: my belief and my love, or, at
least, my affirmation of beauty; and yet they left disgruntled.
Fanatics indeed! Well, at least my contemplation soared and became ecstatic while in that beauty's fanatical but ravishing presence. We all tend toward such fanaticism and dilettantism, playing along the side of the road, forgetting the *end* of the journey;
clutching a partial and puny pleasure, "lest having Him we have
naught else besides," and receiving and giving gifts with no access
to and oblation of the giver.

If we stop short of the deep inner stuff of religion, chances are we'll become either fanatics or skeptics. The deep inner stuff of religion is called the mystical life. It consists primarily of the contemplation of truth. Contemplation is a supremely human and intuitive gaze on truth.

Skepticism cannot achieve this. Its tolerance is forever threatened from within by a vacuum; that is, a negative principle that forbids the skeptic to believe in any truth or to adhere firmly to any assertion as unshakably true in itself. Skeptics are fanatics turned inside out. The only way they can hide their fanaticism is to cut themselves off from the truth. As Jacques Maritain pointed out years ago, such an attempt to live tolerantly in a democratic and pluralistic society is suicidal: no democratic society can be without a practical belief in such truths as freedom, justice, law, and the other tenets of democracy; and any belief in these things as objectively and unshakably true would be nullified by the preassumed law of universal skepticism.

The skeptic asks Pilate's question and copes with the question "What is truth?" in Pilate's way. Because Pilate did not know the answer, he called upon the people and let them decide; and thus in a democratic society it is up to the people to decide, and mutual tolerance reigns, because nobody knows what truth is. The same sort of wide-open, uncommitted, pseudodemocracy is reducing religious life to a shambles.

Some political scientists justify democracy in terms of this barbarous and erroneous assumption: that there is no absolute truth, because if there were, men possessed of *the true view* would impose their vision on others and that would be the end of tolerance.

Be it a question of science, metaphysics, or religion, the man who says, "What is truth?" as Pilate did, is not a tolerant man, but a betrayer of the human race. There is real and genuine tolerance only when a man is firmly and absolutely convinced of a truth, or of what he holds to be a truth, and when he at the same time recognizes the right of those who deny this truth to exist, and to contradict him, and to speak their own mind, not because they are free from truth, but because they seek truth in their own way, and because he respects in them human nature and human dignity and those very resources and living springs of the intellect and of conscience that make them potentially capable of attaining the truth he loves, if someday they happen to see it.

It is nonsense to regard fanaticism as a fruit of religion. Fanaticism is a natural tendency rooted in our basic egoism and will to power. It seizes upon any noble feeling to live on it. In this sense, and in many others, a little religion is a dangerous thing. A fanatic redoubles his efforts to improve and increase his means and his instruments while he has forgotten his purpose and his goal.

There's only one cure for fanaticism and that is more religion; that is, a *full-grown* faith that issues in contemplation: the simple, loving, experiential awareness of absolute reality. For then man realizes the sacred transcendence of truth and of God. The more he grasps truth, through science, philosophy, or faith, the more he feels what immensity remains to be grasped within this very truth. The more he knows God, either by reason or by faith, the more he understands that our concepts attain (through analogy) but do not circumscribe him, and that his thoughts are not like our thoughts. So Maritain concludes that the stronger and deeper faith becomes, the more man kneels down, not before his own alleged ignorance of truth, but before the inscrutable mystery of divine truth, and before the hidden ways in which God goes to meet those who search for him.

So both the fanatic, who confuses the means of religion with the end, and the skeptic, who makes relativism, ignorance, and doubt a necessary condition for mutual tolerance, sin against man (as well as God) because they deprive man and the human intellect of the very act—adherence to truth or contemplation—in which consists both man's dignity and reason for living.

That is why the intellectual life, the first contemplative step in the human adventure, is so important. But it is equally important to do more than that. Taking the second step beyond intellection into deeper realms of faith is crucial.

And so, having taken the first step, take also the advice of the masters of oriental wisdom: See and *pass on*. And remember what

Lao-tzu said: "The most important thing to do is to be." So do your intellectual work, but then, in the words of the Psalmist, "Be still and see that I am God."

*

The purpose of this chapter is to describe the art of contemplation, in the fullest sense of that word, namely, religious contemplation, so it's time to attend to that specifically, and forget about the intellectual life and Jehovah's Witnesses who sweep monks off their feet.

Contemplation is the most complete expression of man's intellectual and spiritual life. And his spiritual life is not just his prayer life or his Sunday leisure or his works of mercy or his sacramental acts. His whole life and all his ways of transfiguring matter are man's spiritual life. This morning, for instance, when I lit my fire and cooked my oatmeal and ate on the porch of my hermitage while I watched the sun coming up out of the woods and shining on the lake, my spiritual life was under way. Earlier this morning at three when I walked over to the other side of the lake to see what was troubling Zorba, who was barking furiously (and this splendid sheep dog seldom does), I was engaged in my spiritual life, as I am now while writing down these reflections. All right, then: It is *this* spiritual life, as well as my prayer life, of which contemplation is the highest expression. It is that life itself, fully awake, fully active, fully aware that it is alive. It is a life grounded in radical amazement, steeped in wonder, and full of awe, immersed as it is in mystery and engaged in intercourse with God. Contemplation is, above all, the loving awareness of God, the invisible, transcendent, and infinitely abundant source of everything. It is directly in touch with this Source, obscurely, mysteriously, but with a certainty beyond the range of reason. It knows God in a "cloud of unknowing" (which is the opposite of not knowing, or ignorance) with a knowledge too deep to be grasped in images, in words, or in clear concepts. The dark knowledge, the luminous night of contemplation, is beyond the highest reaches of any other human effort to know. All other lights are snuffed out momentarily by the dark ray of contemplation but are eventually rekindled in the divine luminosity of a soul blazing with the conflagration of God's love.

We live in harmony with ourselves and with others because we live in conscious union with God. We are able to love all the others only because we know experientially that we are loved by him. We are in touch with the whole cosmos and affirm the intrinsic goodness of everything because we have been touched by him—by him who has no hands but who is Pure Reality and the Source of all that is real. So contemplation is a reaching and a stretching of our whole being toward the ultimately and absolutely real, the Wholly Other.

Contemplation is also a listening to the Word, the Word God speaks from all eternity, reaching its resonant fullness in Christ, so that nothing remains to be said. All has been spoken in the Word, which we must absorb and assimilate into ourselves and into our world as creatively as possible. We are so caught up these days in the narrow, nugatory business of our own solipsistic introspection that we are deluded into assuming that a decisive religious renewal is going on. Well, undoubtedly good things have happened since Vatican II, but bad things have occurred, too. We think we are in a big religious renewal simply because we are asking a million questions. But in genuine religious renewals the voice that is heard in our midst is the voice of God, not our own strident cacophony, and the question raised is God's question, not ours. The universal religious question is the question God put to Adam in the beginning: "O man, where art thou?" There is only one authentic answer to that question, and it cannot be verbalized: *existential presence*. That is what contemplation is: God, out of divine *pathos*, takes the initiative and calls man by name and solicits his sym-*pathy*, his co-operation, and his presence. And contemplative man lives life fully by being, above all other things, alive to God.

The religious question becomes a specifically Christian question at Caesarea Philippi when Jesus asked his disciples: "What think ye of Christ?" They—and we, too—become Christian to the extent that they answer that question out of the conscious depths of

their own being where Christ holds the central position and re-
enacts the mystery of his life, death, and resurrection. In other
words, contemplation is knowing who Christ is, not by hearsay or
by information, but by experience. Peter, one of the disciples
there at Caesarea Philippi, who already shared with Christ his
mystical life, did answer the question experientially; so Jesus re-
joiced and said, "Simon, son of Jonah, you are a happy man! Because it was not flesh and blood that revealed this to you but my
Father in heaven."

Obviously this is vastly different from a metaphysical intuition
of pure essences and abstract ideas. It is the religious apprehension
of God present and active in my life, or the experience of "sonship," as the New Testament says. "For whoever are led by the
Spirit of God, they are the sons of God. . . . The Spirit Himself gives testimony to our own spirit that we are the sons of
God." This personal, loving, experiential awareness of God is a
transcendent gift. It is not the result of human effort. By the
mercy of God and the gifts of the Holy Spirit, the contemplative
comes to know by experience what every Christian believes: "It
is now no longer that I live but Christ lives in me."

It is important to emphasize the gratuity of contemplative grace.
But this concept is most often misunderstood in theory and distorted in practice. The first mistake we make is to assume that it is
a rare gift for a select few. Then most people—those who have
never been very lucky at anything—don't even consider themselves as possible recipients; and the rest of us wait around thinking: "Who knows? Maybe someday God will bless me with contemplative grace and my dull, drab life will be quickened and
transformed." This is all nonsense.

The unspeakably wonderful fact is that the gift has already
been given. All of us are already blessed with contemplative grace,
with the seeds, at least, of contemplation. The one "given" of
the spiritual life is union with God, and this vital union of the
human will (especially) with the Divine Reality is the essence of
contemplation. Until this union is directly perceived by an intuition of the intellect, it remains a "masked" form of contempla-

tion; but if the union is a deep, personal, sustaining influence in the Christian experience of the individual, then it is, indeed, contemplation. Why contemplation is "masked" in most cases is an unfathomable mystery, since God has his hidden reasons. But I would dare say that it is due, primarily, to no lack of grace at all, but to purely natural circumstances, such as the psychophysical disposition of the individual and the nonmystical nature of the environment. In other words, it is the supernatural union that is God's free gift. With the right internal and external circumstances and a particular psychological type of prayerful person, the infused or mystical contemplation simply becomes the connatural concomitant and manifestation of that union.

This may explain the effect of drugs on certain people and their accidental relationship to mysticism. People in general, as E. I. Watkin likes to point out, are temperamentally either transparent or opaque. The transparent personality is more liable to experience the union with God in his will than an equally holy but opaque person. But if the latter comes under the influence of a certain drug, the induced transparency might make him conscious of that union, thus heightening the natural condition for a mystical experience. But drugs do not, under any circumstances, produce a supernatural mystical experience.

The tidal wave of mysticism in Europe in the wake of St. Teresa of Avila and St. John of the Cross is also explained by the same principle. Did God arbitrarily decide to be lavishly generous with his mystical graces to Europeans for a century and then in the next century dramatically withdraw his grace? To suppose so seems ludicrous. It is much more likely that that peak age of mysticism was due to natural circumstances such as the Carmelite influence, the Spanish temperament, and the mystical climate of the Church.

In Chapter 4 I would like to say something about our spiritual lives today in terms of the American temperament. Here I must limit myself to the mystical climate of the Church in the twentieth century. But, first, a personal parenthesis: I am not much impressed with the crowd of Church critics I have been reading and listening to. Their criticisms seem petty, narcissistic, and stentorian. The acrimonious invective heaped on the Church often seems misplaced. Perhaps we need to strike our breasts again and restore the irreplaceable *mea culpa* to our Mass, for is not the central malaise of the Church our own barren experience of the truth? I know it is in my case. Yet I, too, must criticize if I am to be a thoughtful, responsible member of the Church I love. But my criticism must be a discriminating fusion of censure and eulogy; and it must be reverent.

During the Vatican Council I happened to meet Dr. Abraham Heschel, that towering Jewish rabbi, on the street in New York City. I followed him home, and we spent a few hours together. He apologized for the sad mood he was in—a heaviness of heart he could not seem to dispel.

"What made you sad, Rabbi?" I asked.

"My morning prayer," he replied.

"Oh, what were you praying about?"

"Your council."

"Why did that make you sad?"

Heschel answered that question by asking me one: "Father, how many of your bishops gathered at the council are contemplative?" Then *I* got sad.

The rabbi was right to stake the success of the council not on the managerial talents of bishops, nor on the expertise of the theologians, but on whether or not the shepherds of the flock were Christ-men, governed by the gifts of the Holy Spirit, and, therefore, in direct contact with the Living God as he is in himself.

The bishops, of course, were not contemplative enough. The theology of the council was not experiential enough. (I say this without meaning or wanting to denigrate in any way the spectacular achievement of Vatican II, especially in the ecumenical and pastoral spheres. Every human institution is inevitably weak in some areas. The outstanding weakness of Vatican II may be found in the vacuity of its mystical theology.) The life of the Church is still not mystical enough. Until it becomes sufficiently mystical, the doctrinal and liturgical changes will remain inept, and all the modernizing, streamlining, and Protestantizing will be of no avail. In fact, all this face-lifting may do more harm than good because it deludes us into thinking that a real renewal is going on—with no *metanoia*, no radical change at the center either of the person or of the Church, no experience of God. Without that experience we will have new slogans and better clichés perhaps, and ever more sophisticated and disguised idolatries; but no profound and permanent change of mind and heart.

After years of research, Aldous Huxley concluded that in our long human history we have discovered only one proven way of changing human behavior permanently. Preaching and teaching don't do it; religious practices don't do it; contemplation, and nothing else, does.

But the mystical element of the Church is the least recognizable aspect of her doctrine and life. This is obviously and tragically true despite the good leadership of Pope Paul VI and despite the fact that mysticism is the Church's longest, deepest, and most fruitful tradition and the lifeblood of her body. Baron Friedrich von Hügel distinguished three elements in religion: the mystical, the rational, and the institutional. But the rational and institutional elements are not essentially or in themselves religious. Religion is in its essence wholly and solely the mystical, or, as E. I. Watkin says more correctly, the experiential element. Without mystical experience, at least in its essential will-union aspect, religion is a corpse. Theology is merely the conceptual interpretation and liturgy the ritual embodiment of that central Christian experience.

The council has not noticeably rectified the mystical failure of the Church. Countless young people starving to death in our Western churches, homes, and schools where they are being fed stones instead of bread, leave this world of theological abstractions and ethical principles behind them in search of the deep mystical tradition they've heard or read about in Hinduism, Buddhism, Sufism, and Zen. Many religious orders (even some Carmelites) have become less contemplative, more feverishly and fruitlessly active. In the name of renewal many monasteries and convents have been turned into something like country clubs or inner-city clubs complete with "kites, kocktails, and ticky-tack," as an architect friend of mine in Columbus describes it. Nuns, who, by their vows of chastity, poverty, and obedience, entered into a publicly professed *bridal* relationship with Christ, are now admittedly embarrassed by the public recognition of that fact. Men and women, gifted and trained to be different, are now making titanic efforts to make no waves but to be placidly absorbed into the leveling egalitarianism of a waist-high culture. Since the council I have watched a new diocese take shape. It was built on the policies of public relations and ecclesiastical safety rather than on the prescriptions of the Gospels: mystical relations with God and the principles of sanctity. Is not this to build on sand? Is it not, in fact, to rebuild the recalcitrant world that takes the place of the Kingdom of God, the world to which Christ laid the ax?

A Christianity that is not basically mystical must become either a political ideology or a mindless fundamentalism. This is already happening, as Alan Watts, one of the most original philosophers of the century, popular interpreter of Zen, and author of a spate of books on the philosophy and psychology of religion, and many others have pointed out. In the absence of the *eternal now* of mystical theology and the "virtue and power that go out from him" when touched in mystical experience, theologians are forced to project the secret, the gnosis, the mystery, of the Church into the future or maybe even now *if* things were different, and so theologies of the future—and of a political and revolutionary nature—begin to appear. (Not that they are bad or wrong. There is much that is good about them, but the complex reasons for their appearance here and now should be carefully scrutinized.) As for the other extreme substitute for mysticism, the fastest growing religious bodies in America are fundamentalist. And, as is evident in both these trends, where there is no authentic mysticism there is apt to be Biblicism (an inordinate attachment to the Bible). I, for one, am inclined to agree with Dom Aelred Graham and Alan Watts that biblical idolatry is one of the most depressing and sterile fixations of the religious mind.

There is an old Jewish story that makes the point trenchantly. A young fugitive, trying to escape the enemy, had convinced the people of a small Jewish village to hide and protect him. But when the soldiers came and threatened to burn down the village and kill every man, if the fugitive was not handed over, the people got frightened and asked the rabbi what to do. The rabbi was caught in this awful dilemma. So he went to his room, took the Bible, and started to read, hoping to find an answer. After a while his eyes fell on the words "It is better that one dies than that the whole people be lost." So the rabbi closed the Bible, called the soldiers, and handed the boy over to his enemies. The village celebrated with a big feast. But the rabbi returned to his room with mixed feelings. At that moment the prophet entered and asked, "Rabbi, what have you done?" The rabbi said, "I handed over the fugitive to the enemy." Then the prophet said, "But don't you know that you have handed over the Messiah?" "How could I know?" the rabbi replied anxiously. Then the prophet said, "If, instead of reading your Bible, you had visited this young man just once and looked into his eyes, you would have known."

That's what I mean by Biblicism: an exaggerated devotion and superstitious attachment to the Bible that undermines our own dignified and mature responsibility to cope creatively with the exigencies of the human adventure. Without contemplation men can only look back in anger or forward in fear and fantasy, but cannot look into the present reality with loving awareness.

What the Church embodies and should, therefore, convey is Christ's own experience of the Godhood. By being christened we come into our own realization of divine sonship—and that is the mystical experience. Baptism is the sacramental sign of this happening; and to some degree it effects what it signifies. It ratifies and celebrates the inception of the existential Christian fact: the experience of God in Christ. The fullness of this experience is symbolized and celebrated in the Eucharist. Whenever anyone plunges into this sacramental experience with fully human deliberation and love, he enjoys an incomparable peak human experience;

so much so that any other peak experience would become utterly superfluous.

The Incarnation establishes without a doubt, once and for all, the *given-ness* of union with God. We do not have to attain divine union. We do not have to climb out of our messy flesh into the pure Spirit of God. God has become man. Our flesh is his flesh. We cannot strive aggressively to possess God, nor can we earn or deserve union with God. The spiritual life is the affirmation, appreciation, and realization of the union we already enjoy. *Yes, we* say, and *amen* with our whole lives to the pathos and agape of God. One is free, of course, to ignore God's life in us and to reject his love. That is how we condemn ourselves. And we call this self-condemnation the judgment of God—and rightly so.

To say that we are already united to God is one thing; the experiential realization of it is quite another. The whole symbolic structure of religion is meant to make this possible. The purpose of religious exercises and ceremonies is to make our faith grow to the point where, having followed all the pointing fingers to the end, it transcends the means and rests in God. Nothing is too sacred to be detached from. St. John of the Cross says that if we are going to be attached to God, we must be detached from all that is not God. If we belong to anything or anyone except God, we are enslaved. God's sovereign claim is unconditional; so must be our surrender. "It makes little difference whether a bird is tied by a thin thread or by a cord," says St. John of the Cross in *The Ascent of Mount Carmel*. "It is regrettable to behold some people, laden as rich vessels with wealth, deeds, spiritual exercises, virtues, and favors from God, never advancing . . . which requires no more than a sudden flap of one's wings to tear the thread of attachment."

I am not crazy about this age I happen to live in. I suspect that a hundred years from now historians will regard our times as a particularly unremarkable and flabby epoch. But there is one outstanding and saving feature of this cellophane age, and that is the Dark Night of the Church. The purgative aspect of the Dark Night can be terrifying, and usually is when the individual or the institution has not been very mystical. But purged we must be in the Dark Night, for there is no other entry into the mystical life: the experiential realization of union with God. There are multifarious forms of the Dark Night. If only they were recognized as such and understood in their psychological and theological perspectives, there would be a lot more live men and communities and families around. I will delineate and specify all this concretely in Chapter 9. Right now I want to call attention to the Church's unique mission at this historical juncture: to move with reckless abandon, in total poverty and courageous obedience, into the Dark Night. This is a perilous venture, but if the divine challenge is rejected, the Church will have nothing to say to the world. If accepted, then the Church's dogmatic and doctrinal symbols will lose force and be shattered until, and in order that, their inner content may be known.

Only the reckless lovelife of the Church can save the world. Trying to hang on to God and to possess him religiously (spiritual ambition is as bad as material ambition) is as ridiculously impossible as attempting to live a full life in a miserly way. The more miserly we are, the more life evades us and the sooner we die of worry. The more we try to contain God and tame him, the more he eludes our grasp. He will not be tamed, not by our theologies, our states of mind, our feelings, our experiences, our books, our creeds, our sacraments, our churches, nor by any human effort. We think we are being very religious and marvelously renewed when we find a place for God in our world. But God has no place in our world. He *is* the place of the world. We fit our world into him and his Kingdom. Not vice versa. God does not fit. As Abraham Heschel says: It may be within man's power to seek God, but it is not within his power to find him. As long as we try to grasp God, we shall never realize him. In C. S. Lewis's magnificent myth *The Chronicles of Narnia*, which enthralled me during sleepless nights in the hospital and which I heartily recommend to everyone, the children are both mystified and miffed by the behavior of Aslan, the lion, who both saves them and staggers them. And so the children keep saying to one another: "We must remember that

Aslan is not a tame lion." We must remind one another that our God is not a tame God. He is not nice; he is not a buddy or a mascot; he is not an uncle. He is an earthquake. "It is a terrible thing to be caught in the hands of the Living God," the New Testament reveals.

Hopefully, it is now ineluctably clear that *the nub of the art of contemplation is artlessness or naïveté.* There is no method or formal technique for realizing union with God. To realize union is, in fact, a very simple and childlike affair. We complicate the whole business by our egotistic compulsion to achieve, to attain, and to accomplish. Did not our Lord say that his yoke is easy and his burden light? Meister Eckhart said it best:

> He who fondly imagines to get more of God in thoughts, prayers, pious offices and so forth, than by the fireside or in the stall: in sooth he does but take God, as it were, and swaddle his head in a cloak and hide him under the table. For he who seeks God under settled forms lays hold of the form while missing the God concealed in it. But he who seeks God in no special guise lays hold of him as he is in himself, and such an one "lives with the Son" and is the life itself. [Sermon XIII, in Pfeiffer's *Meister Eckhart,* Vol. 1., p. 49.]

We become ingenuous, less rigid and self-conscious when we recognize God as the active agent of our spiritual lives. He loves, hounds, woos, holds, and captivates us. All we can do is respond. Realization comes and the possessive will surrenders itself when we feel spiritually bankrupt and are thoroughly convinced that struggle and squirm as we may, there is no escape from the love of God.

Being gratefully receptive and keenly responsive is a far cry from the nullity of quietism. Eschewing or at least minimizing contemplative methods and techniques is meant in no way, as will be seen in subsequent chapters, to repudiate a balanced asceticism or a discipline of life, but to avoid any kind of rigid methodology. It was just such a methodology that, in our own day, had been turned into a pharmacology of mysticism—"mist-to-schism" freaks swallowing pills and turning on.

The only way you can possess God is to be possessed by him. The only way to enjoy him is to let him go. The only way to be heightened is to be humbled. The only way into the light of day is through the darkness of night. The only way to be divinely enriched is to be so poor you don't even have a god. God, through the work of his hands (creation), takes hold of us; not the other way round. It is our grasping, acquisitive nature that spoils things. The beauty you leap upon dissolves under your dead weight. Clutch the splendor of flame and you get burned; pluck a flower and it dies; scoop water from a brook and it flows no longer; snatch the wind in a bag and you have dead air. The more bloody determined you are to capture life and hold on to it, the more life will elude you and your own self-asserting effort imprison you. To enjoy any living thing—fire, water, air, animal, vegetable, human, God himself—we must let go of it. When we free it from our grasp, we, too, become free. In detachment is our liberation; and in our liberation the earth is hallowed and God is glorified.

Divine union is realized not by programs and practices cleverly devised or solemnly prescribed and religiously adhered to, but by a life of creative fidelity lived fully without bargaining, compromising, or holding back. In other words, realization of union with God is the graceful result of authentic human experience: life, deeply participated in and intelligently interpreted.

The rhythm of religious experience is made up of an awareness and a processive affirmation that are interconnected: an awareness of the given relationship, which comes from creation itself, and from God's initiative within us; and a practical affirmation of this relationship, which is personally accepted with gratitude, and then willed, and hence renewed, deepened, and transposed to a new level—from the ontological to the spiritual—and leads to our communion, not as a merely natural being, but as a personal being, with God. It is through this intimate and existential claim or passionate affirmation (the willingness to suffer life) that the *given-ness* of union with God becomes interiorized and personalized. This is necessarily so, since man is not only a ravished recipient of cosmic disclosures but a passionate pilgrim of the Absolute.

Chapter 2 – A Long Loving Look at the Real

The salient aspect of the spiritual life, as I tried to make clear in the first chapter, is a given one: union with God. We are endowed with Spirit from on high. There is no way that we can become identical with God. But we can become deified. We do not become totally human until we become partly divine. God became man, as St. Athanasius said, so that man might become God. It is God (who is love, and love is diffusive) who takes the initiative, unites himself to us, keeps us alive by his creative and attentive presence, and with no violence, but with the gentle fury of an irrepressible and invincible love, touches us where we are most free and invites us, seductively, into the intimate and infinite lovelife of the Trinity.

What we need to do is sensitively recognize who we are—brides of the bridegroom (that is why Greek, Latin, and Spanish all use feminine words for soul: *psyche, anima, alma*)—and be aware of what is going on: we are being led to the bridal chamber. In other words, *realization* of the union with God we already enjoy, responding in every way we know how to the overture of God's love, adoringly recognizing his presence in a broken but marvelously transparent world—that's what the spiritual life is all about. As the first chapter points out, the loving awareness of God is a gradual enlightenment of mind and enlargement of heart that corresponds with a *perceptive appreciation of things and their significance, a love participation in their mystery, and a long-view interpretation of their meaning.*

This threefold human response to a diaphanous world is a description of the contemplative life of every man that begins with the simple savoring of a seashell, a hazelnut, a sunset, a playful saluki, a roaring lion, a human body, a soulful presence, moves awesomely and reverently through the resonantly beingful orchestration of the whole world, and comes to rest in the wisely passive "monstration" of the pure intuition of God.

It is this decision for, and rendition of, a full life, rather than any formal method or technique, that prepares the soul (the body-mind, if you like) for the experience of God. Such a preparation, though vital and vigorous and amazingly effective, has not the slightest trace of pecksniffian introspection or sanctimonious self-consciousness. There is no zany quest for experiences as such but rather an awakened sense of how the whole joyful-painful adventure of living, whether on the crest or in the troughs, is in itself the God experience.

Mystical experience is far more like a man learning to walk than a man learning to fly. An isolated peak human experience is more like the periodic refreshment of a man's *vacation* than like the processive daily task of a man's *vocation*. Peak experiences are those occasional mountaintop views that encourage us to press on toward the end, to the mystery at the end of the journey, glimpsed and foreshadowed along the way. The daily pressure of the Spirit, the persevering forward movement, the whole experience of life along the way, on the heights or in the hollows—this, and not the sporadic peak experience, is the essence of the mystical life.

There is a great deal of interest today in mysticism; there is also plenty of confusion. Much of the confusion is due to a failure to distinguish adequately between experience and sensation. A person's experience is what he has lived through; it is cumulative and communicable (though not entirely at peak instances). Sensation is personal, confined, and incommunicable—something felt rather than experienced. The distinction is necessary: so much of the talk today about "religious" or "love" experience is really talk about sensation. The distinction also is important: sensation has nothing to do with the relatedness, communion, and *binding together* of religion. Accumulated experience means knowledge, sometimes wisdom; it produces experts, sometimes wise men. Sensations may be intense, exciting, interesting, and shocking; they are never cumulative. Experience takes us out of ourselves (ecstasy); sensation affirms and emphasizes self. Whereas the person who enjoys or suffers an experience makes history, the person in quest of sensation merely has a "happening" or a flutter in the diaphragm.

Obviously then, despite all the glib talk and mind-blowing antics, we live in a sensate culture and are woefully bereft of experience. A quick look at so many of the art galleries, theaters, films, novels, growth centers, spiritual fads, modern theologies, and "groovy" churches is all we need to see a desperate quest for sensation valued more than experience.

Experience is a hard concept to tie down. One thing is clear. It cannot mean what it did for the classical empiricists who made it the equivalent of sense data. We need the larger view of our own day according to which *experience* may be defined as *the whole range of the self's active relationship with the other*. Self and Other are the two poles of experience. You cannot know the self independently of its interaction with the other. I understand myself as a body through my relationship to other things and as a person in my relationship to other persons who appeal to "me" for a unique response. If these levels of interaction exhausted my experience, there would be no need to talk about God. But there is a level of the self, a dimension of experience that does definitely transcend these particular preoccupations. I am real over and above my interaction with particular things and persons. It is on this level that I am finally rooted and utterly responsible. Here I am a solitary: alone with the All.

At this pinnacle of selfhood the Other whom I have direct experience of is God. I find myself appealed to beyond all particular engagements. I find myself loved beyond the limits of all created being. This love defines and identifies me and calls into question all my particular relationships. This is the One I take with absolute seriousness, the One to whom I am ultimately answerable.

When I respond from the depths of my being to this transcendent appeal, I embody God's presence in my life and am divinized in the process. When I reject or ignore this deepest dimension of my being, I am decentered, an enormity that disturbs the whole universe and leaves me unhinged.

The experience of God is the ground of and one with my experience of myself. His nearness puts me close to myself. He is, in fact, as the mystics say, closer to me and more myself than I am. I cannot offend myself without first offending him. When I give up my own convictions, I betray him. If I become a saint, he is realized and glorified in my wholeness.

*

The only way to know God is by experience: the way the lover knows the beloved, the spouse knows the spouse, the friend knows the friend, and the wise adventurer knows life. There is no other way. We can get to know him in a hundred different ways. But the only way to know him as he is in himself is by experience.

To experience something—anything—we need to enter into it in a threefold way: by perceptive appreciation, participation, and interpretation.

1. By a *perceptive appreciation* of the thing itself: to perceive, to recognize, to see things as they really are. To *worship* is to see the real *worth* of things and respond to him who gives them their value. To worship in spirit and truth is to catch the splendor and glory of lilies and lions, of mud and men, not just the temple, and so to discover and respond to the presence of God everywhere, not just in Jerusalem. To see that the world is crammed with God, that everything is a sign, a symbol, and a sample of him who summons us to be and to contemplate: this is to imitate God who worked until the seventh day, then looked on what he created and found it all very good.

Looking directly at reality, affirming the intrinsic goodness of things, coexperiencing with God the totality of being in a single acorn or a blade of grass or an alley cat—that can be, and often is, a high point of the human adventure. Wise men, Orientals especially, are unimpressed by the trumpeted and truncated renewal going on in the Western churches. They look with pity on our feverish activities, our frantic rearrangement and reorganization of religious trumpery, and ask so piquantly: "But have you changed the inner eye?" Lao-tzu gives us sage advice:

> The five colors can blind,
> The five tones deafen,
> The five tastes cloy.
> The race, the hunt, can drive men mad
> And their booty leave them no peace.
> Therefore a sensible man
> Prefers the inner to the outer eye:
> He has his yes, he has his no.
>
> 　　　　　　　　　(*Way of Life.*)

Without this special kind of eyesight we shall never discover the inner splendor of things or their important connections. Herb Gardner in *A Thousand Clowns* (Henry Hewes, ed., *Best Plays 1961–62*) describes this eyesight in a marvelously simple and secular way. Uncle Murray tells what he wants for his nephew:

> I just want him to stay with me till I can be sure that he won't turn into a Norman Nothing. I want to be sure he'll know when he's chickening out on himself. I want him to get to know exactly the special thing he is or else he won't notice it when it starts to go. I want him to stay awake and know who the phonies are. I want him to know how to holler and put up an argument. I want a little guts to show before I let him go. I want to be sure he sees all the wild possibilities. I want him to know it's worth all the trouble just to give the world a little goosing when you get the chance. And I want him to know the subtle, sneaky, important reason why he was born a human being and not a chair. I will be very sorry to see him go. The kid was the best straight man I ever had. He is a laugher, and laughers are rare. I mean, you tell that kid something funny—not just any piece of corn, but something funny, and he'll give you your money's worth. It's not just funny jokes he reads, or I tell him, that he laughs at. Not just set-up funny stuff. He sees

street jokes, he has the good eye, he sees subway farce and crosstown bus humor and all the cartoons people make by being alive. *He has a good eye.*

The wise man is the experienced man who lives with his eyes and his heart wide open, full of reverent wonder and radical amazement. But he is not equally open to everything. He perceives a hierarchy of being, a gradation of value. He discriminates, distinguishes, and discerns the spirit. He also recognizes and confronts the demonic dimensions of being, the mystery of iniquity. He knows that life is short and he is limited, so he sifts, selects, and chooses just that much of the raw material of this world that he knows he can infect with his love and transfigure with his spirit. He lives so wakefully and expectantly that little of value escapes his notice, and whatever is worthwhile evokes his loving attention. He sees the things of this world as rare treasures or as things never seen before.

Taking a long loving look at the cherry, delighting in its roundness and redness, is as important to him as eating it. Man does not live by bread alone—certainly not by the consumption of bread alone—but by the contemplation of bread. One hunger is satisfied by the consumption of a meal; a deeper hunger is satisfied by the contemplation of a meal. The perception of the social, aesthetic, and spiritual values involved, for instance, in the luscious sight and smell and taste of artichoke or avocado and the enjoyment of fine fellowship and good talk. When a husband ceases to take long loving looks at his wife, then no matter how much he copulates, his love diminishes and the marriage begins to fade. If I am pulled by multiple desires into the fancied future, I cannot see how much good fills the here and now. If I am driven by compulsion, I am not free to wait, to look around lovingly and longingly until I find what will not merely tease, taunt, and tantalize me sporadically, but will hold and captivate my focused attention and feed forever with prodigious prodigality the wild, passionate fury of my hunger.

Drivenness and crowdedness scatter our perceptions so disparately that our lives become helplessly fragmented and we are inexorably reduced to uncollected dispersion and spiritual torpor. A driven man is enslaved. He becomes a robot, an automaton. Even if what he is driven to is of inestimable value, for instance his own perfection or the salvation of others, he is still shackled by his drives. He must learn to act freely, thoughtfully, lovingly. Most of our sins are due to thoughtlessness. We don't have bad wills; we intend to be kind, but caught off guard, we lose our perspective and behave abominably. What we need is insight. But insightfulness grows in stillness and tranquillity. It needs lots of leisurely time (holy repose) and uncrowded space. Most of us will have to stop doing half the things we do in order to do the other half with the liveliness of faith and the contagion of love. Henry David Thoreau offers first prize to the man who can live one day deliberately. Because we do too many good things, the one important thing remains undone. "Mary has chosen the better part." If our lives are crowded with things or even with people, we will not notice any one of them sufficiently to make an act of love. Sometimes deliberately, sometimes subconsciously, we crowd our lives for that very reason: to respectfully avoid the awful, exhausting, ego-annihilating act of love.

If our experience is so disgracefully limited and embarrassingly thin, it is due primarily to our lack of insight, our failure to see how beautiful things are. Things deceive us by being fantastically more real than they seem. We are such hurried, harried people, in touch with real things with only one third of our minds, that the essential gist of things escapes us. We reduce everything to merely this and hardly that when in fact everything is, in its own way, *all that.* Such is the basic insight of the Upanishads, one of the great religious literary treasures of the world: *Tat tvam asi*—Thou art that. There is a Christian nonpantheistic way of understanding this: "Thou art Christ, Son of the living God." All the stunning ramifications of that incarnational fact issue in a comparable Christian insight.

In the light of this central revelation our various forms of thoughtless reductionism seem hideously irreverent and irresponsible. A man says self-excusingly, "I'm just doing my job" or

"I'm just carrying out orders" or "That's the way things are," and the evil consequences, the pain and the suffering, are incalculable.

It is this kind of careless reductionism—it's just a black man, a bum, a criminal, an old man, a cripple, a mental case, or it's just air, water, a bunch of trees, a vacant lot—that has reduced our nation to a highly sophisticated and blissful shambles.

My brother recently chided me for wasting days and nights in fruitless prayer and search for a dog lost in the woods. "After all," he said, "it's just a dog, and you've got pressing things to do." I've got to make him understand there's no such thing as *just a dog*. Every dog expresses uniquely the dogginess of God, a quality of God that can be found nowhere else. God is that dog lost in the woods. While he is lost, though I may not and need not find him, there is no other way for me to seek God here and now except by seeking the lost dog. The search cannot be fruitless nor the time wasted. The dog, lost or found, cannot be loved too much. Love may be spoiled by mawkish sentimentality or egotistic instrusions, spoiled precisely because of the diminution of love; but love itself has no excess.

The U.S. military says "it's just a dog" and kills the thousands of dogs that comforted, consoled, and delighted American servicemen in Vietnam during that senseless war. Applying the same principle, the same military power committed one of the worst atrocities in the history of the world by slaughtering hundreds of thousands of helpless, innocent, and (often) friendly civilians in Vietnam, insouciantly justifying itself by saying it was just "collateral damage." This is one example of the euphemistic barbarism we have come to accept in our sophisticated stupor.

Human degradation and the violent desecration of the earth will continue unchecked until we discard all our respectable blindfolds, put on the mind of Christ, and see things rightly: the manifold in the One, everything in the Eternal Now. A perceptive appreciation of things, which is the first indispensable element of experience, evokes reverence; and reverence is a key virtue; in fact, I think it is the keyest of all virtues. If I were delicately and distinctively reverent to myself, to others, to everything, to God, I would never sin. Sin is always an act of violence: twisting and distorting something or someone out of shape and out of harmony, and thus disrupting the universe, for my own private profit, pleasure, and purpose.

2. In addition to a perceptive appreciation, then, the second essential element of human experience is *participation*. It is not enough to see, to observe, to be a detached spectator. Life must be *suffered*. Experience is not the result of contrived "happenings" but the fruit of a man's total immersion in existence. He doesn't strive for neat little experiences. He simply spends himself, coping creatively with the exigencies, tragedies, and serendipities of the human adventure, suffering life with unconditional and unselfconscious abandon. It is imperative to recognize with Gabriel Marcel that life is not a series of problems to be solved but a mystery to be lived. Only by becoming a passionate participant in life can man enjoy a sense and knowledge of reality gained from direct intercourse and be led by this contact with the real into vital union with the ultimately Real, God himself. Exploration into God requires one kind of experience of every human being: the penetration of the real.

It is not enough to look at the woman; if we are to know her, we must dwell with her, share life with her. Pitying the poor man is not enough; we must share his poverty. Visiting the sick is a good deed half done; we must feel the pain. Mourning the death of a departed friend or relative is fitting; but we must also feel his presence more keenly now than before his death. "There but for the grace of God go I" is a kind gesture toward a criminal; but it would be more appropriate and compassionate to say and to feel: "There, hidden in that man's public crime, are all my private sins." People who announce preposterously that they don't like cats have never dwelt with a cat or been inundated with the feline quality of God. Hunters who kill deer for sport and raccoons for coats can't imagine what it is like to be a deer or a raccoon, or for that matter, what it is like to be the Creator of the deer and raccoon; or what it is like to be, as every man is, the custodian of God's creation, whose duty and privilege it is to take care of the universe. By that I mean: to help the universe realize goals that it cannot realize itself. W. H. Auden said: "I think we might have a decent world if it were universally recognized that to make a hideous lampshade, for example, is to torture helpless metals. And every time we make a nuclear weapon, we corrupt the morals of a host of innocent neutrons below the age of consent."

We tend only to have vicarious relationships with the real (book knowledge) and so deprive ourselves of the stuff of life as we move desultorily into a derivative existence. Some people, mostly young, have begun to break out of this dehumanized condition. But we have a long way to go. We need to get into the sun, the air, the water, the woods, the sand. We have to get into the squalor of the city with enough light and love to transfigure it. We have to get into the game and into the dance. Otherwise we will suffocate and die.

An analogy: You are responsible for fifty teen-agers. So you gather them together and put them in the parish hall and tell them to dance. You go for a cup of coffee. You return and witness this scene, a typical one: four or five girls dancing in the middle of the hall, and all the guys hugging the walls. Well, that's a pathetic but, I think, fairly accurate image of the Church. At the heart of the Church there are a few live ones—the saints on earth—participating, doing the Christ dance, re-enacting the mystery of faith, the birth-death-resurrection of the Everlasting Man. The rest of us are hugging the walls, cuddling up to the institution and the structure, smugly and securely "doing our thing" on the threshold of the Church; and from that safe distance we watch and discuss the action at the center of the Church.

A few years ago when James Kavanaugh with a characteristic yawp left the Church and the ministry, I was invited to engage him in a national television debate. The television encounter never took place, but in thinking about our common problems, I dare say the crucial problem of the day, I tried to put my finger on it by nefariously changing the title of Kavanaugh's book. He called it *A Modern Priest Looks at His Outdated Church*. My new title was *Mod Priest Sits Out Date with Church*. That's his problem. If only he had been in there dancing! It's my problem, too. If only I could plunge indefatigably into that wild and exhilaratingly wonderful Christ dance, I would not be unduly disturbed by the petty problems that proliferate and are perpetuated on the edges of the Church, and I would not suffocate from the monumental trivia that pile up and pollute the suburbs of reality. There is no salvation on the outskirts of the Church. Defections abound there. So do betrayals.

Some years ago Father Timothy and I visited the Bernard Leddy family in Burlington, Vermont. It is a very convivial family and very Democratic. In the course of the evening, Father Timothy, a Carmelite friar and friend of mine, who is a tiny, gentle man, softly mentioned that John Kennedy, who was running for the presidency at that time, was no saint. Well, the reaction was like a thunderclap! Father Timothy became the pitiful object of powerful Democratic scorn. He could hardly remember what he said to deserve such a frightful response. With a twinkle in her eye Johannah Leddy comforted him by whispering in his ear: "No one *wades* in my house." How true! And that is why it is one of the great human homes in America! And there is no wading in Christianity either. Refreshment and renewal come from plunging into the deeps.

We must come in or go out. All the way in—where the fire is and the sacrificial lovers are all aglow with the Spirit. Remember Dom Marmion, renowned Benedictine abbot and spiritual writer? He said the difference between the saints and the rest of us is that they plunge boldly and daringly into the fire of God's love and come out burned but incandescently and utterly transfigured. We put our little finger in, get slightly burned, and spend the rest of our days circling the fire at a niminy-piminy gait, far enough away never to be burned again but close enough to be warmed by it. Such lukewarmness and mediocrity even Jesus could not stomach.

On the back cover of his album *John Wesley Harding*, Bob Dylan comments on man's apathy (passionlessness) and disinclination (despite his fatuous similitudes) to pursue the truth:

a full liberated life. According to Dylan's oblique parable, three kings suspect that a man named Frank has the key for understanding the new Dylan record. The three kings find Frank, who admits that he is, indeed, the key to the knowledge they seek. "Well then," asks one king in a bit of excitement, "could you please open it up for us?" Frank, who all this time has been reclining with his eyes closed, suddenly opens them up as wide as a tiger. "And just how far would you like to go in?" he asks, and the three kings all look at each other. "Not too far but just far enough so's we can say that we've been there," admits the first king. (James Douglas, *Resistance and Contemplation*, p. 46.)

Such a trenchant appraisal of our paltry pursuit of the truth! We run from star to star, seek out the latest celebrity, far less enlightened than we are but made notable by the media, listen to the foolish and frantic banter of those sickening talk shows, saturate ourselves with and become utterly desensitized by the unrelieved and indisceet exposure to Muzak and newzak—we prefer to be diverted by this enormous stupefaction than to be thoroughly and thrillingly engaged in the exploration into our own transcendent inner truth. So instead of participating passionately in a full-bodied life, we remain dumb, dull spectators on the periphery.

3. The third essential element of experience is *interpretation*. It unifies and integrates the multiple items of the experience, providing a processive pattern of meaning, a purpose, and an ultimate fruition. Interpreting the experience is like making a collage. It sees all the connections and possible relationships and gives a single focus and shape to a hundred different vibrations and relations. It achieves certainty, continuity, and integrity by directing human forces onward and upward precluding the isolation and aberration of creative and imaginative human thrusts toward the transcendent.

The fruit of experience, the wholeness of life, requires good interpretation. A good football quarterback is a good interpreter. So is the live motorcyclist. He scans the field or the road, recognizes half a dozen problems at once, makes quick and appropriate judgments, moves deftly and adroitly, and he is in the clear. And so is a good man with a lively faith. He copes with the exigencies of life quickly, gracefully, and creatively. He is thus a moral man. Though he is thoroughly cognizant of the sudden, inextricable eruptions of a brand-new experience into the moral life of man that need to be freshly evaluated, he does not abandon in a panic or a rush of enthusiasm the permanent basic structure of morality. And whatever may be said about dynamic truths (the only kind that modern philosophers and theologians recognize), the good interpreter admits of static ones, too, in order to give a proper account of the reality we experience. He needs a conceptual scheme to describe the frame of reality needed for everyday discourse, and far more so, for our experience of the moral order.

Not very long ago Father John Courtney Murray, the distinguished American theologian, reminded us that nowadays we must realize that truth is a historical affair, involving all the relativity of history and the subjectivity of human beings. Truth is therefore, he insisted, an experiential affair. Theology, then, should be concerned not so much with how certain we are, but with how truly, deeply, and experientially we understand traditional affirmations of truth.

A hearty *amen* to that. But let me be quick to add: a lived faith is steeped in truth, informed by reason; a lively faith is rooted in experience. We needed the emphasis on "historical consciousness" by such recent authors as Murray, Karl Rahner, Bernard Lonergan, and Michael Novak. But that, too, can be exaggerated and often is. Dom Aelred Graham in his last enigmatic book, *The End of Religion,* sharply criticizes this historical preoccupation of Catholic and Protestant theologians. I tend to agree with much of his criticism, as I also agree with his British compatriot, the brilliant Jesuit scholar Martin D'Arcy, who refuses to relegate "static" truth to unhistorical habits of thought in past ages. A doctrine must be permanent, and grow nonetheless. It must acquire a *dynamic* quality without losing its *static* virtue. I love the dark and chancy gamble of life, too. But why must we associate *certainty* with a stick-in-the-mud attitude? Rigidity, yes, is a veritable straitjacket. But certainty often characterizes towering human beings. One of the most remarkable and impressive qualities of Christ was his certainty regarding his mission; one of the most noticeable and depressing features of modern churchmen is their uncertainty regarding the mission of the Church.

The interpretation of an individual's or a society's experience cannot afford to be facile or flighty. There is the temptation to be trendy. But the quickest way to become old hat is to climb onto the latest bandwagon. If you wed the spirit of an age, you soon become widowed. To return idolatrously to the altars of antiquity is egregious folly. But it is no less ludicrous to turn contemporaneity into a god. No matter how potent and persuasive an ideology is, it is silly to stake one's life on it. The average span of an ideology is about five years. Marxism and Freudianism lasted longer but took new forms. We keep running around in crazy circles reformulating the philosophies and theologies of our predecessors instead of philosophizing and theologizing wisely and uniquely ourselves; or we amuse, retard, fixate, ourselves by replacing rusty old ideologies with shiny new ones instead of transcending the ideological plateau altogether and living by the pure, undiluted, and undivided power of the Logos.

Insofar as a Christian—or Christianity itself—completely accommodates and fully identifies himself with a particular socio-cultural context, he smothers himself and nullifies his purpose in the world. If the Church gets swallowed up in the secular world, it cannot speak to the world. So many religious men and women, clergy and lay alike, seem uprooted today and are frantically in search of a culture with which to identify. Johann Nestroy, the nineteenth-century Austrian comic playwright, says that there are three kinds of souls in the world: "There are some men who go to pieces when their mistress leaves them. These are little souls. Then there are others, bigger souls, who quickly replace their mistress when she goes. But the really great souls always have a replacement waiting in the wings." Read "culture" for "mistress" and my point will be clear: There is no paucity of "great souls" in the Church today. And that of course is too bad. Nestroy's "little souls" would be better off: bereft of old securities but unable to console themselves with new ones, they might be ready to enter the Dark Night and live by faith.

American sociologist Peter Berger (author of *Rumor of Angels*) seems to corroborate my tentative view that the little souls are very few and so the Church is skirting the Dark Night opportunity. The search is on for new cultural partners with which to enter some form of Christian union. "The list is long: the youth culture, the counterculture, black culture, various romanticized versions of a future culture that is to ensue from this or that revolutionary liberation . . . once more I think it is necessary to affirm the transcendence and the authority of Christianity over and beyond any cultural constellation in history, present or future, 'established' or still striving for 'establishment.'" Peter Berger thinks the Church has listened too long with uncritical adulation, if not idolatrous intent, to "modern man." I concur. Modern man needs to be spoken to, needs to listen to the Word of God spoken with authority by the Church; like the Virgin Mary, "modern man" needs to treasure up all the things he hears the Church speak of and ponder them in his heart. "Could it not be," Berger says in his *Rumor of Angels,* "that modern consciousness, far from being the pinnacle of man's cognitive history, may rather be the result of an impoverishment in a man's grasp of reality?"

The perennial fidget to be in fashion can have a detrimental effect on more than one's ease of mind. "Fashion in artistic and intellectual theory is always fluid, new catchwords are born every year, and nothing is more pathetic in its desuetude than the intellectual or social chic of yesterday," according to author Paul Horgan. Or as Anthony Burgess said: "For God's sake stop talking about relevance. All we have is the past."

The only valid interpretation of my experience is myself. But no man is an island, so there is no such thing as an isolated human being. I am linked to all others and am irrevocably rooted in the Wholly Other. So my experience must be interpreted in terms of this intricately interlaced pattern of existence. I must ask: What does modern man have to say to the Church? And though I doubt he will have much more to say than he said so far, I must remain open to the possibility. A more enduringly important question is: What does the Church have to say to modern man?

I assume what the Church says to the world will be based on criteria of truth, not of sociocultural market research or public relations. I am not asking the *modern* Church, but the Church ever ancient and ever new. Its most recent message is essentially the same as its most ancient. The irrecusable wisdom of the ages is what is important. So I interpret my experience in the context of the long living tradition of the Church, not just the recent past, but the whole past alive in the present. The *long view* is a must.

We have appropriately disparaging names for the man whose horizons are limited: parochial, provincial, insular. We need a corresponding term for temporal limitation, which is a very common and very damaging defect. It spoils a great deal of contemporary theological writing and discussion, both traditional and progressive, preoccupied as it is with merely a recent hundred years or so of tradition which is such a small fraction of the life of the Church and of mankind. Baron von Hügel insisted that his niece Gwendolyn not confine herself to spiritual books but read history, especially pagan classical literature. He wanted her to sense the richness of God everywhere:

> The all-important point, I think, at each step is to feel how rich, how inexhaustible, how live it all really is! That is why I am trying to get such words as "Rome," "Athens," etc. to mean a great rich world to you. I hate all the notions that there is no value in anything that is past—that the only value is in what we got now. That cuts us off, it gives us no base, it leaves out the richness and soundness of the great traditions. I want to teach you through all those gigantic things, the martyrs, gnosticism, skepticism, that atrocious thing the 18th century. I want you to learn about the great souls that lived through all those tracts of time. [Maeder, Michael, "Being Human— a Study of Friedrich von Hügel," *Sisters Today*, Dec. 1972, pp. 183–97.]

I must say that I agree very much with G. K. Chesterton's remark about tradition and the past when he says: "Tradition means giving votes to that obscurest of classes, our ancestors. It is the democracy of the dead. Tradition refuses to surrender to the arrogant oligarchy of those who merely happen to be walking around." It may be that we are so much the product of our time that we don't even realize we are. We have become too absorbed in it, as some Christians in previous times and places have been absorbed into the trivia of their time, so that we are caught up in things that really are of no importance at all, except insofar as they seduce us from the center of our lives and make us forget our real tradition. What real tradition? The Christian humanist tradition, which is based on text after text, on doctrine after doctrine, on life after life, on saint after saint, all in eccentric rebellion against the easy lapse into the concentric spheres of a self-centered, self-satisfied society.

> We shall not cease from exploration
> And the end of all our exploring
> Will be to arrive where we started
> And know the place for the first time.
> —T. S. Eliot, *Four Quartets*

Tradition is dynamic, selective, and creative. What memory is to the individual, tradition is to the community. If a man loses his memory irrevocably, he loses his humanity. If a community forfeits its tradition, it gives up its life. Tradition is the past that endures to shape and enrich the present. How shimmeringly clear this was in that exhilarating film *Fiddler on the Roof!*

Stuffy, stodgy conservatism is not traditionalism. It is pathetic immobilism. It is an inordinate attachment to a historical past now dead or to the status quo, a comfortable rut that takes the place of tradition. We must not allow the misuses or distortions of tradition to blind us to its rich potential as a means of transcending the limitations of our experience. Detached from the immediate past but steeped in the living tradition of mankind and the Christian community, we will move graciously and unperturbably through experiences, crises, and upheavals of all kinds, sustained and steadied by the deepening recognition of one fact alone: God loves us. That is the utterly simple articulation of the central experience of mankind.

Chapter 3 – The Whole Man

An in-depth experience of life deliberately lived and not just managed—that's the solid stuff of mysticism. It involves pain and pleasure, prose and poetry, doctrine and insight, work and play, sorrow and joy—the whole mystery of life. Conscious immersion in the mystery equals mysticism.

Much of this mystical life involves us in human actions that are shockingly useless, that seem to be devoid of purpose or meaning. And we won't tolerate that, not even in the subhuman realms of being. How loudly we boast that all those seemingly pointless plants and animals have a purpose since *man* eats them, and even the stars produce a planetary home for man. This bit of arrogance is based on the old notion of nature as a hierarchy with man at the top. But our modern awareness of the whole of nature as an ecosystem contradicts that silly idea. Otherwise, we would be compelled to say that man has a purpose because he provides food for maggots and rats.

What does it mean to be gainfully and meaningfully employed? Does it mean staving off death by reproducing ourselves, perpetuating the unreal world, and thus exposing our children to the techno-barbaric juggernaut? Does it mean keeping the factories, freeways, suburbs, and big corporations going, buying appliances on time, and becoming more and more securely insured? Does it mean eliminating the poverty, racism, and warfare of this generation to be replaced by the poverty, racism, and warfare of the next generation ("the poor you will always have with you")? Does it mean racing pell-mell into space and gnashing our teeth in despair at gaps we can never cross?

Or is meaning found elsewhere? Perhaps it is: in the repudiation of the whole ego performance, including the political games, the ideological foofaraw, the technological madness that breeds the poverty, the racism, and the warfare.

We stake our lives on our purposeful programs and projects, our serious jobs and endeavors. But doesn't the really important part of our lives unfold "after hours"—singing and dancing, music and painting, prayer and lovemaking, or just fooling around? And isn't that what we are really after? But how meaningful is wasting time? How practical is making love? And what is the purpose of painting a landscape, singing a song, or gliding aimlessly round and round the room?

There is no need to justify these useless activities by imposing artificial meanings: "therapy," "relaxation," "food for thought," "preparation for work." They are simply useless, which is no mean quality to possess. Some of our finest human acts are useless: praying and playing, for instance. Some of our most wonderful creatures are equally useless: a hippopotamus is an obvious example; or a saluki: you can hardly train or control salukis—they are such delightfully wild and intractably noble dogs—but they are one of the most beautiful creatures in the world. ("What are salukis used for?" asked a retreatant at our Nada Ranch. We wanted to say, "nothing," but replied, "Beingfulness" instead. The gentleman learned firsthand himself.) The ancient ruins of Rome and Athens are as useless as they are attractive. And hovering St. Louis so gloriously and welcoming you to the West so alluringly that you almost don't notice the ugliness of East St. Louis there is an exquisitely splendid arch, an architectural triumph that is utterly useless.

There is a marvelous precedent in the Gospels for our useless actions, creatures, and creations. Judas was infuriated with Mary Magdalene for wasting precious ointment in such a reckless gesture of love. But Jesus commends her. It is easy now, even for "practical" men, to see why. The ointment could have been sold and the poverty of a few Jews could have been momentarily relieved. Instead millions of men all over the world are being inspired time and time again by the useless, poetic gesture of love.

It seems that loons fly and dive and swim for the sheer pleasure of it. Their laughter resounds through our woods and lakes. Humans who live as wildly and laugh as uproariously as they do are often called "crazy as a loon." Porcupines don't have a care in the world, and no purpose; they don't even *mean* to punish playful dogs with their quills. Giraffes are finding out what it's like to have a tremendously long neck. Humans, too, are finding out what it's like to be human and to do human things such as thinking and loving, laughing and crying. Purposes are what we concoct in our heads. Experience is what it feels like to be human and knowing why.

A very human thing such as music can hardly be said to have meaning. If you have to get something out of it, you spoil it. If all those horns in the second movement have to be explained, it ruins it. A good musician delights in sound itself, in ordered melody and harmony for its own sake, with no attempt to say anything. In music meaning coalesces with experience.

The universe is like that: an orchestration of the one Word God speaks from all eternity. It is the music of the spheres, and nothing in heaven or on earth is left out. It is the canticle of love emanating from the ground of all being and reverberating through the cosmos. Infinitesimally tiny segments of that grand orchestration have been isolated, abstracted, studied, reproduced, and preserved in our libraries, churches, universities, and other monuments of our "purposeful" life. These entombed fragments of live moments of the human adventure offer no substitute for the wild, precarious exploration itself.

Benedictine monk Sebastian Moore has spoken significantly of this *meaning* in the *New Christian* (April 3, 1969):

> It seems to me that we have to be altogether more radical here. The very notion of meaningfulness as predicated of a man's life is, I think, essentially descriptive of a man's achievement. It refers essentially to what we manage to build. It refers to the process whereby we step out of our sheer intolerable weakness into a human world having shape and dignity in spite of our absurdity and

death. What I call the human lie is never wholly absent from it.

To talk of "meaning" as emerging at the heart of our absurdity and weakness is a serious confusion of language. In the more limited sphere of thought about things, the price we pay for making sense of things is a process of abstraction that must leave behind "the empirical surd," the sheerly experienced. This is more than the *price* of making sense. It is what making sense is. Well, I in my immediate feel of the human worldly condition am the sheerly empirical. If I say that *I*, in this fated mortal condition, "make sense," I lie. And yet I hunger. I am I. I cannot endure to be "left behind" as an empirical. But I hunger for something other than meaning.

The Gospel, and it alone, interprets this hunger to me in the declaration of its appeasement. That declaration is, irreducibly, the statement that God loves me. And this love of God in Christ Jesus is not something I step into with dignity. It is that in which I am lost.

And that is why the community in Christ is not a ceremonious and dignified community in which the members owe their mutual recognition to a common language. It is an agony of mutual involvement, and the agony is one, whether it is that of exposing ourselves to those who do not yet understand, or whether it is that tremor of eschatological oneness that is sometimes given to us. It is always a creative dying. The taste of Christ ranges from the death in which enemies are loved to the death in which we sometimes touch together the hint of resurrection.

The realities we experience are concrete—this pain, this pleasure, this event, this woman. As long as we are thoroughly engaged in the act of loving this woman, bearing this pain, enjoying this pleasure, we are not intellectually apprehending personality, pain, or pleasure. As soon as we begin to do so, the concrete realities become mere instances or examples: we have now switched from them to that which they signify. We can either taste the concrete thing and forgo clear knowledge or clearly know and forgo the taste; or more accurately, we lack one kind of knowledge because we are in an experience or lack another kind because we are outside it. While thinking we are cut off from what we think about; while tasting, touching, loving, hating, we do not clearly understand. Who can study pleasure during nuptial ecstasy or comprehend repentance while repenting or analyze the nature of anger while roaring with indignation?

How do we become possessed by the Whole Truth—perceived and conceived, experienced and interpreted—the truth that makes us free? The myth is one partial solution. For instance, when I lay in the hospital reading *The Chronicles of Narnia*, I was not learning anything about Christianity. I was tasting the whole Christian mystery. What I was then tasting turned out to be a universal principle. But the moment I stated that principle later on in reflective articulation I moved into the ordinary workaday world of abstraction. It was only while I was receiving the myth as a story that I experienced the principle concretely. I was feeding on reality, not truth. The truths came later when I translated the mystery of the *Chronicles* into dozens of abstractions. Myth is not, like truth, abstract; nor is it, like direct experience, bound to the particular. It is the bridge that connects the world of discursive reasoning or intellection with the vast continent to which we really belong.

The whole sensorium, alive and alert to reality, keeps us in touch and in tune with the world. We cannot live on abstract ideas. Visual images do not reveal enough of the world to us. Being in touch requires a highly developed and refined sense of touch. The refinement I am thinking of seldom characterizes the "touchy-feely follies" of so many of the sensitivity groups and growth centers that abound now in the United States. Feeling is certainly not the cornerstone of mysticism (Christ is; see Paul's letter to the Ephesians 2:20), but it is a touchstone of our connections with reality and must therefore be recovered if we are going to live whole lives. When I go out and lie on the ground by the edge of the lake and listen to the waves on the shore and the wind in the trees, something happens that is almost impossible to explain. Let me just say: Everything is *here* and *now*. When I am left unselfed, disarmed, and reborn by a deep and total encounter with another human being—none of the "here's where I'm at," "letting it all hang out," "telling it like it is" nonsense, but utterly rent and spent in the altruistic outpouring of my small, limited self into the separate, circumscribed individuality of another—together we plunge into intercourse with everyone. Nothing genital, but a presence and a union so incredibly intimate that it is ineffable. In this sense of *presence* Christ's prayer for everything and everyone is answered: "May they all be one: as Thou, Father, art in me, and I in Thee, so also may they be in us, that the world may believe that Thou didst send me."

It may seem that I am doodling and dallying instead of zeroing in on the deep sense of contemplation, the substantial quiddity of mysticism, and the art of contemplating in the earthly Kingdom of God, established by Christ. But all that has been said thus far has been said within the context of the Christ world. There is no other authentic realm of being from which to speak. The unsacred, unchristened world of secularism is the unreal world condemned once and forever by Christ. Our primal sin since the Carpenter from Nazareth demolished the foundations of the old world and established a brand-new world on a whole new axis is to go on acting as if that never happened, basing our lives on pop religion and power politics and military-industrial pressures instead of the Sermon on the Mount, the Crucifixion on Golgotha, and the vindication of that shameful death in the Resurrection of Christ. Reality is now rooted and redirected. There is a radical reorientation. Christ didn't tidy up that old world. He brought it to a screaming halt and made all things new. Christ is the new Adam: not a religious genius introducing a new religion: and what he re-formed out of the human stuff of the old world was not nicer people with better morals, but brand-new men. By his revolutionary life, his radical reappraisal of human values, and his free and deliberate choice of death, he undid in us the religious habit of millions of years. The cross cures man from his age-old religious addiction to convenient gods of his own, and to man thus freed it says, "Here is God." ". . . the crowds were appalled on seeing him—so disfigured did he look that he seemed no longer human" (Isa. 52:14). And here is the real world—issuing in the freedom and exaltation of risen man but steeped in agony, absurdity, weakness, and sin.

What sociologists are calling a post-Christian world is really a *pre*-Christian world—the massive effort of many societies to live by principles and values of a condemned world, the world before Christ or the world that is not his Kingdom. (It is not Judaism that is condemned. What is Christianity without Judaism? It is the city of man un-Goddened that is the pathetic object of God's wrath.) Despite prodigious technological achievements, economic prosperity, educational reforms, medical advances, and religious renewal, this world, the biblical "city," is doomed. This doom is reflected in the million human distractions and the monumental despair of our schizoid society. How silly to take comfort in the untiring efforts of Church and state to readjust and rearrange the ecclesiastical and political furniture when their respective worlds are severed from their vital source and center. Such frantic correctional patchwork makes as much sense as running a race in the wrong direction or redirecting a stream that is poisoned at its source. The present feverish flurry of humanitarian activism and peripheral tidying-up is equivalent to rearranging the deck chairs on the *Titanic*—one way, indeed, of getting a better view going down.

These multiple ways of *going down* "with honor" always seem to take one of the many forms of secularism. This is particularly regrettable as well as pathological when it happens to the Church: when religion, in the name of relevance, *seeks to adjust itself to the times*. The leader becomes led. Jacob Needleman, philosopher-psychologist of San Francisco State College, asks very pertinent questions in *The New Religions*:

> As church and synagogue turn to psychiatry, the scientific world-view, or social action, are they not turning toward what has failed and is failing? And has not the

very failure of these non-religious enterprises shifted the common mind back to a renewed interest in the religious? Men turn to religion and find, to their ultimate dismay, that religion turns to them, to their sciences, their ideas of action and accomplishment, and their language. This is what is known as secularization: the effort by religion to be "relevant," to "solve" human problems, to make men "happy."

Modern man does not need a little more organization or sociability. He needs a savior. He needs basic, not complete, answers for the basic problems of his existence that no social organization can provide. It is depressing to see Christians pumping up a Christianity that is no more than social humanism at a time when the men of our day are beginning to discover the inadequacies of all such merely humanistic stopgaps and are beginning to hunger for God. It is a distressing spectacle to see man asking for God from a Church that no longer gives him God.

The real mission of the Church is to transform men into God, into Christ-men, or more accurately, to create and foster such a lively, human atmosphere, a climate so pregnantly divine, so significantly related to the Wholly Other, that the same Spirit of God who erupted in Jesus and turned him into Christ the Lord will rise in us and form the contemporary Christ in us. The Church has lots of jobs to do, but one mission: the formation of saints. And if the Church has failed its mission (and I maintain that it has; see my final chapter), it is, ironically, because it has done its jobs too well, expending its vital forces and exhausting its manpower in efforts only remotely related to its central divine mandate: Pray and get the Gospel to every creature.

Why has the Church failed? Why is it that we today, with all our refined spirituality and our scientific study of religion, our recent fascination with oriental wisdom and techniques and mind-expanding drugs and exercises, our accumulated experience of Christian doctrine and insight, our superior psychological and pedagogic methods, our plethora of religious literature, our retreats and workshops, and countless apostolic programs and projects—why is it that we, with all this machinery at our disposal and such a mass of goodwill, are not saints? I venture to say it is because we are not human enough. We dare not let ourselves become human beings. We assume that we are born human and thus remain apathetic about our major project of existence, which is to become in fact existentially human by taking conscious hold of the amorphous human stuff we were born with and giving it, creatively, a marvelously distinctive human form. We are not responsible enough for the shape our lives take. We let too many things happen to us. Perhaps we need, like Thoreau, to go to the woods to live life freely and thoughtfully.

The Virgin Mary is the supreme human example of this superb kind of responsibility. And she did not need to go to the woods but remained right on the spot where she was. There she stubbornly refused to let too many things happen to her—to be frazzled, fragmented, dispersed, a victim of superficial circumstances and conditions. She was rooted, integrated, stilled, a "woman wrapped in silence." Though caught at the center of a tempestuous series of cataclysmic events, she never panicked. In harmony with herself and all others she was at peace: steeped in the tranquillity of order. She was peaceful but not apathetic. All the passion of the whole Jewish race welled up in her. The wild, fierce, and irrepressible cry of Israel, its insatiable hunger for God, was summed up perfectly in the flesh and blood of this young maiden and expressed unequivocally in her Magnificat. Precisely because she refused to be pummeled by the unsifted and unselected elements of life or to be inundated by trivia, she was prepared to have the most wonderful thing in the world happen to her: "Be it done unto me according to your Word." It was her total yes to the devastating demands of God's love; it was her valiant fiat that ushered in the *new man* and the real world, and made all things new. One of the best books I know of on Mary is *A Woman Wrapped in Silence*. Here Father John W. Lynch presents her precisely as an earthy mystic.

> "This was a woolen garment that she wore
> About her tired shoulders, and the hands

That brushed the weight of hair from her brow
Were roughened with the water jars, and knew
The feel of sunlight and the form of bread." [pp. 4–5.]

Wherever we are, whoever we are, the responsibility for the integrity and beauty of our personalities cannot be shirked. I must get up each morning, take life into my own hands, and put my own distinct, unique, and unrepeatable stamp on it. I must freely decide to create the mood of the day rather than let the circumstances and conditions of the day rule my life. With my spirit (the breath of God in me) I will transform the raw matter of my life and make it beautiful. That is my human vocation and my moral duty.

*

Grace perfects nature. That means that whenever and wherever God finds a good decent human chap he sanctifies him (or her). We do not lift ourselves up by our own bootstraps. We respond to God's initiative and ultimately abandon ourselves adoringly to his dominion. But God does not do violence to his creatures. He forms them and fills them, all right, but according to their nature. Neither does he act in a vacuum. He needs in us appropriate and viable human dispositions. God will do nothing with us unless we let him. We let him when we are humanly disposed. *We become more humanly disposed as we grow in the loving awareness of God through a reverent relatedness to everything.* That's the Christian adventure. That's the way to become holy: by becoming whole. But this does not mean that we go around busily and self-consciously relating. This is a trendy thing to do today, a reaction against isolationist forms of spirituality. I have two friends, both married men, who are caught in this trend. They came out of an orgiastic sensitivity session one day really high, inebriated by their own exuberance. They went to visit a young woman, a mutual friend. They invaded her privacy, deluged her with words, offended her with sentimental slosh, and crushed her with bear hugs. When she did not respond in kind, they told her that she was "hung-up" and left her drained and disgusted.

Equally foolish is the clumsy effort to bludgeon one's way into personal encounters or delicate moments of human intimacy. Poor old Monsignor Clancy, who has been feared and revered all these years by his loyal and devoted people, is now, suddenly and sadly, just plain old Pat to the swinging jet set of the parish. I am out-raged by the people who call Father Louis Merton "Tom," and I am revolted by strangers who call me "Bill" (certainly no friend would). A bishop who hardly knew me used to write me "Dear Bill" letters. I had an occasion to write him a critical letter that could have been the beginning of a real friendship. Ever since then his letters begin with "Dear Father McNamara"!

Such a fatuous and insensitive effort on the part of sensitivity freaks to relate intimately with everyone is ludicrous and kills the very possibility of entering into a profound, sincere, and self-donating act of holy communion.

Relatedness is indeed the key to holiness. We cannot sanctify ourselves. We may have the best technique in the world, the most ardent will, and the purest intuition: still there's no way to pull it off on our own endeavor. Only God can sanctify us, which is what he does when he draws us into a reverent in-depth relation-ship with anyone or anything.

The idea of relation enters the very notion of person. Philoso-phers who have not the slightest notion of the Trinity, where the persons are subsistent relation, share this view. The "I" of the person of its very nature calls for the "Thou" of the I-Thou rela-tion. It is mainly by its relative opposition to the "Thou" of an-other that the "I" of the subject comes to realize his self-awareness as a person. Still, the person is not merely relation. There is under the relation an abiding, enduring reality unfolding through pro-cessive relationships.

Once you accept this view of personality, you know that real knowledge of another must be intuitive rather than conceptual, experiential and not abstract. Only by intuition do we really know a relation, not by conceptual knowledge. A relation is *toward something* rather than *something*. We do not *have* a relationship but *are* in relation. So the knowledge of this being in process is dynamic rather than static. But since there is some knowledge of the *thing* involved, there is at least a modicum of static knowledge, too; but it is incapable of capturing the *quality* of person. Through intution the luminosity of the person is experienced.

An I-Thou relationship is not a merging or a fusion. (When two companies merge or two drops of water fuse, only one remains.) It is a union of solitaries. The poet Rainer Maria Rilke describes love as being two solitudes that protect and touch and greet each other. The contact is born not of the minimal conceptual knowledge, but of the direct experience involving a sensible and intellectual intuition of the mysterious and literally ineffable and inexpressible other whom we address, awesomely and intimately, as Thou. In this global intuition, knowledge and love combine in one beingful experience, leaving us somewhat dumbfounded but marvelously integrated and ennobled human beings.

This is what it means to become the image and likeness of God: to develop the graced capacity we have for altruistic love relationships. God does not have a social life, a community, a trinity of persons. God *is* social life, community, trinity. No one of the persons of the Trinity has or is anything in and by himself. Each one is entirely for the other and is constituted in being by eternal relatedness to the other. The Trinity is the altruistic lovelife of God. We are truly human to the extent that we do in fact become, existentially and not just theoretically, the living image and likeness of God. It would be disastrous to conclude from this that Godliness or holiness requires a constant round of encounters, meetings, "relating" sessions, and endless talk. On the contrary, only silent solitaries are capable of enjoying communion and building community. A silent solitary is not a dumb caveman or a withdrawn zombie but a Christ-man who speaks with authority.

The axiom about grace perfecting nature is the only theological principle I know that explains the appalling and embarrassing inefficacy of the sacraments. According to Catholic doctrine, they are powerful sources of life and do effect what they signify. They undoubtedly do have regenerative power—but not by magic or divine intrusions. The sacraments are *human ways* of coming into contact with healing or enlivening sources of divine life. The efficacy or degree of divinization depends upon the humanness of the participation. If, for instance, I partake of the Eucharist with inhuman dispositions (callousness, resentment, pious conventional routine), I can expect bad rather than good effects. That is why St. Paul warns us against participating frivolously. A striking contemporary example of a sacrament badly confected is penance. The predominant form of this sacrament in confession has been for a long time, and frequently still is, outrageously inhuman.

"Grace perfects nature" does not only mean that God brings to perfection a properly disposed person; God also thrives in any human event or situation that is thoroughly human. The sacrament of penance needs to be humanized. It is highly significant, I think, that all other ecclesiastical and pastoral changes that occurred in the last few years transpired with or after much discussion. But the practice of frequent confession, even though prescribed by Canon Law, simply stopped with no discussion at all: the form was obviously so inhuman.

Though it is possible and sometimes ideal, the dark, spooky box is not ordinarily a humanly appropriate place for confession. If the confessor is going to be judiciously gentle, tender, insightful, and firm, then he should be able to look into the eyes of the penitent. If the penitent is going to be deeply self-revealing, then he or she ought to choose a confessor very carefully and then go to him at the right time and the right place. Both penitent and priest must be eminently human if the sacramental grace is going to fructify. The penitent must accept some of the responsibility. People should be determined not only to get the negative effect of penance, which is liberation from the horrendous burden of sin, but also the positive effect, which is transformation into Christ. In other words, every time someone has confessed, he should be thinking more like Christ, loving more like Christ, and acting more like Christ.

I hope it is clear now why these first chapters are premystical rather than mystical. If the human foundation is weak, the mystical experience will be spurious. A group of nuns came to our contemplative center in Sedona, Arizona, to spend the summer in prayer. Our role is to set the stage as humanly as possible for the gracious experience of God. So I spoke to the sisters about the art of being human. One of these ladies took offense, pointing out to me that she came to the desert not to learn how to be human but to have a prayer experience. Her failure to see the connection between humanness and prayerfulness prevented her from praying out of her own inner truth. Her preoccupation with having a prayer experience made prayer that much more difficult. Can you imagine the apostles saying to one another, "Let's go get Jesus and have an experience"? You can look back on a singularly moving event and say that was an experience. But if you set out to have an experience, it is bound to slip through your fingers. I worry about many of the pious people that are so jubilantly "into prayer" these days. They seem to be prayer-conscious rather than God-conscious or God-intoxicated. Remember what St. Anthony of the Desert said: "He prays best who doesn't even know he's praying." The secret of the spiritual life is not so much the art of contemplation in and for itself, but the art of integration of life and contemplation.

Chapter 4 – The Pleasure of His Company

A few years ago Jacques Maritain published some optimistic reflections on American life. He wrote in *Reflections on America:*

> There are in America great reserves and possibilities for contemplation. The activism manifested here assumes the aspect of a remedy against despair, and masks a hidden aspiration to contemplation. If in American civilization certain elements are causing complaints or criticisms, they proceed from a repression of the desire for the active repose of the soul breathing what is eternal. . . .

To wish paradise on earth is stark naïveté. But it is
better than not to wish any paradise at all. To aspire
to paradise is man's grandeur; and how should I aspire
to paradise except by beginning to realize paradise here
below? The question is to know what paradise is. Paradise consists, as St. Augustine says, in the joy of the
Truth. Contemplation is paradise on earth, a crucified
paradise.

I share Maritain's optimism to a degree. I see, however, two
monstrous obstacles that pertain to all men everywhere but especially in America: narcissism and utilitarianism.

The mood and manner of the day is heavily and contagiously
narcissistic. Like Narcissus, instead of being unselfconsciously but
significantly related to the Other, we pine away at the edge of
the lake or the mirror-gazing upon our own reflection. This may
seem like an anomalous characterization of what seems, at a
superficial glimpse, to be a socially sensitive age. But every weak
age in the history of mankind has been—and this is a telltale
symptom of an internal vacuum—obstreperously and ostentatiously
social.

Self-realization is the driving force of the day. Everyone is
asking, "What's in it for me?" "What do I get out of it?" Op-
portunism prevails. Permanent commitments are out. What seems
comfortable and expedient is good. Most of the priests and
sisters who marry, though variously motivated, are almost always
victims of narcissism. The dominating influence in most cases
known to me has been the *I* and the *me* and the *mine*—never
Christ, almost never the Church. It is particularly significant,
I think, to note the number of theologians, priests, and religious
who leave the broad vistas and immense horizons of the Catholic
Church, priestly ministry, and religious life for the soothing and
stroking, the swinging and burping, received in the warm, secure
arms of an overweening psychologism.

A chap just left my presence who exemplifies this trend.
He, his wife, and their child were overnight guests. At Mass the
following morning I spoke of how damaging it is to turn love

into a pragmatic deal, which is what we do when we work it out in the following way: we are in the world to find personal fulfillment. This is our basic need. We cannot find this fulfillment in and by ourselves. We need others. They are the object of our need. So we combine and pool our needs, thus fulfilling each other, giving each other satisfaction, helping each other to realize ourselves as fulfilled, that is, as gratified. Then I went on to criticize this package deal in a marketing society where love is mistaken for satisfaction of mutual needs and the scratching of each other's back.

Our guest, ex-Jesuit, ex-priest, and now, of course, a clinical psychologist, challenged my thesis and insisted that "man is nothing but a felt-need; man himself is an itch." Well, there you are. That's what I mean by narcissism. And the woods are full of such ex-religious "itches."

The younger Freud seemed to feel that every infant, invaded by the outside world of reality, either repressed his narcissism or replaced his narcissistic and pleasure-oriented ego with a "reality-ego." The older Freud seemed to have changed his mind, and concluded that perhaps the individual infant adopts external reality as a kind of extension of his narcissistic ego and thus seeks to make reality into a pleasure-gratifying phenomenon. Thus, whenever the child experiences external reality as unpleasant, he returns his libido (erotic love) to himself. But when he can gratify his ego with higher levels of satisfaction, his narcissism and external reality tend to merge as extensions of one another. He does not identify himself with the world, since his mastery of language, his body, and his nervous system accentuate the distinctiveness of each. But he breaks off his cathexis of that world only when it ceases to gratify his ego. And so the healthy child (as well as the healthy adult) expends his energy in turning the world into what he wants it to be. This pleasure-seeking principle is what Freud calls primary narcissism, and on it he stakes the well-being of both child and adult. At times, the helpless infant and the neurotic person feel incapable of changing external reality, and thus return their cathexis to themselves and seek to live under the rule of what Freud called secondary narcissism—that is, real selfishness.

There is a very recent theory based on Freud (e.g., Henry Malcolm's thesis in *Generation of Narcissus*) that the youth of today, thanks to the hard work and permissiveness of their parents, technological conveniences, and their own affirmation of self through their ego-oriented drive toward pleasure and fulfillment, enjoy a kind of utopia rightfully inherited from their parents. Although parents have succeeded with their children because they now enjoy the pleasures and comforts and leisure their parents worked for, they have not managed to change their society. Hence it is only by rebellion that this generation can live in the utopian style it deserves as evolved and liberated human beings. So the theory goes.

My own experience, as well as what I have learned from the experience of others, contradicts this modern theory and belies the facts the theory is trying to explain. Far from being pleasure-mad, the average child (including the college student) does not even seem tempted to what you and I have once called pleasure. He doesn't seem to have the stomach for it. No appetite. He wants facts, not pleasure. The idealistic and hedonistic child is still the exception. Most young people, like their elders, are soberly devoted for the most part to what you and I call work.

This remains true despite the fact that the twentieth century has not only realized, within reason, its dream of leisure time but has also supplied the riches with which to fill it. What has man done with the copious treasures and leisure time so bountifully bestowed upon him? There is a compulsion to multiply the riches and to *achieve* something in leisure time. And so we are driven by the neurotic compulsion to work. Both the quantity and the quality of leisure are governed by work; in other words: when does my work allow or require it, and how does leisurely pleasure fit into and ready me for my work? We are compelled to read for profit, to have parties for contacts, go to lunch for contracts, play for therapy, drive to get there, gamble for charity, go out to build the community, stay home to rebuild the house.

Our leisure hours are as frantic and busy as our work hours and therefore meaningless—meaningless enough to drive some of us to drink, some of us to the hospital, and all of us to the beck and call of the marketplace.

Although twentieth-century technology has given us the time to be leisurely, it has not changed our conviction that labor alone is worthwhile. A nostalgia stirs in us: the haunting possibilities of pleasure—if only we would take the time to do nothing. But we are compelled. Pleasure is postponed by more and more laborious preparations or promises that are never kept or are eventually corrupted by unexpected profitable (and therefore, we say, unavoidable) intrusions. We are ruled by profit.

How human are we if we do not resist being pushed? If we cannot rebel during working hours, then we should, at the very least, when work is over, leap to our leisure with wild and reckless abandon, with singing and dancing and shouting in the streets, with irrepressible joy in escape from everything intolerable. I am still looking for a lively city in this young but moribund country of ours. I have worked—not just visited, but worked—in every state in the country except Alaska. I have not yet found a palpable and pulsating kind of vitality that ought to characterize a live city. New Orleans and San Francisco are more alive than most, but even they are pallid and their pleasures piddling.

Why should a young country so blessed with natural resources and extraordinary opportunities be so lifeless, almost lugubrious? Because of its principal law: Only useful activity is valuable, meaningful, moral. Activity that is not clearly useful to oneself or to others is worthless, meaningless, immoral. When you hold, as most of us do, that value depends entirely upon utility, then you miss some of the liveliest and most beautiful human experiences. What twentieth-century man holds to be important and worthwhile is usefulness, the profit that may be extracted from an experience or a possession. When he does not put his every working hour to useful pursuits, he is socially a poor citizen. When he wastes time on acts that rest in the understanding alone, he is morally guilty.

This is called utilitarianism. It is a philosophy. It is *our* philosophy of life. It is, I believe, the chief source of our American malaise. We owe the original formulation of utilitarianism to Jeremy Bentham, a British philosopher. We owe the best criticism of this philosophy and of its "workaholic" devastations in our American society to Walter Kerr, who in *Decline of Pleasure* charmingly and mordaciously exposes the weaknesses and falacies of this philosophy and its desolating effects on American culture. To him I am indebted for much of this chapter. I regard his insights and suggestions crucial in our imperative need to develop a contemplative life in America. I cannot improve on what Mr. Kerr has written so masterfully but simply want to pinpoint and accentuate his central theme.

It may be one of the monumental ironies of history that Bentham should have founded his system on the principle of pleasure. Pleasure, he said, was the sole motivating force that drove men into all their activities. The pursuit of pleasure and the avoidance of pain govern us in all we do, say, and think. A moral act is one that gives us pleasure; an immoral act is one that gives us pain. The amount of pleasure any object of action possesses may be reckoned by its *utility*, by its usefulness, and by no other norm. Bentham's identification of happiness with utility, of pleasure with profit, is absolute.

For Bentham all pleasure is circumstantial: the pleasure that may be taken out of a thing and the pleasure that might be taken in it. The poor thing itself is either raped or invaded. And the pleasure seeker is exhausted rather than refreshed by his pleasures. A hundred years of this has left us in a complete funk. We have lost the habit of *unprofitable* pleasure. Charles Darwin, who at one time in his life was so pleasured by music that his backbone shivered, recalls the tragic decline of pleasure in his *Recollections:*

> I have said that in one respect my mind has changed during the last twenty or thirty years. Up to the age of thirty, or beyond, poetry of many kinds, such as the

works of Milton, Gray, Byron, Wordsworth, Coleridge, and Shelley, gave me great pleasure, and even as a schoolboy I took intense delight in Shakespeare, especially in the historical plays. I have also said that formerly pictures gave me considerable, and music very great delight. But now for many years I cannot endure to read a line of poetry; I have tried lately to read Shakespeare, and found it so intolerably dull that it nauseated me. I have also almost lost my taste for pictures or music. Music generally sets me thinking too energetically on what I have been at work on, instead of giving me pleasure. I retain some taste for fine scenery, but it does not cause me the exquisite delight which it formerly did. . . .

This curious and lamentable loss of the higher aesthetic tastes is all the odder, as books on history, biographies, and travels (independently of any scientific facts which they may contain), and essays on all sorts of subjects interest me as much as they ever did. My mind seems to have become a kind of machine for grinding general laws out of large collections of facts, but why this should have caused the atrophy of that part of the brain alone, on which the higher tastes depend, I cannot conceive. A man with a mind more highly organized or better constituted than mine, would not, I suppose, have thus suffered; and if I had to live my life again, I would have made a rule to read some poetry and listen to some music at least once every week; for perhaps the parts of my brain now atrophied would thus have been kept active through use. The loss of these tastes is a loss of happiness, and may possibly be injurious to the intellect, and more probably to the moral character, by enfeebling the emotional part of our nature. [Walter Kerr, *Decline of Pleasure*, pp. 67–68.]

You can imagine what was happening to less agile minds if this was happening to Darwin.

We are robbed of the pleasure of leisure not by sheer toil alone, but by the yen to invent and convert, as well as by the temptation to do good. Samuel Johnson would become infuriated when his conversations were curtailed by a busy man. He claims to have met in his life only one forerunner of the modern busy man. This busy man was no executive. He was a missionary-reformer. "John Wesley's conversation," according to Johnson, "is good, but he is never at leisure. He is always obliged to go at a certain hour. This is very disagreeable to a man who loves to fold his legs and have out his talk as I do."

Today we are far more wedded to and crippled by utilitarianism than Darwin was. And we are far more prone to the rigid dutifulness of Wesley than the lavishly wasteful love of Christ. If our religious renewal were really vital, it would focus on *being* and thus require a fantastic waste of time. As it is, it stakes success on *doing* and so is driven into feverish and meaningless activities. The colleges and universities are now so afraid of the *useless* nature of the fine arts that they manage to describe their subjects as the "Communication Arts," accenting a scientific commitment and implying that their interest is in decibels and wavelengths rather than poetry or drama.

It's incredible how we've chained ourselves to this gloomy philosophy. Oscar Wilde and his late-nineteenth-century clansmen were no match for Bentham, but at least they didn't take that dour doctrine lying down: "Let me say to you now that to do nothing at all is the most difficult thing in the world, the most difficult and the most intellectual." Besides, "industry is the root of all ugliness." Wilde did not reunite art and society; he raises art above society: "We live in an age of the overworked, and the undereducated; the age in which people are so industrious that they become absolutely stupid. And, harsh though it may sound, I cannot help saying that such people deserve their doom. The sure way of knowing nothing about life is to try to make oneself useful." (From *Decline of Pleasure.*)

These flashes of bravado were not enough to save art from its useful doom. As Walter Kerr says: "This is fine art rampant and confessedly irrelevant. The position is admirable in its energy and regrettable in its resignation. Art has in a single haughty breath given the challenge and given up."

Even the novel has had to become "socially significant." But even in decline art has some incurable good habits. It cannot help but reflect the spiritual life the world actually possesses. It is the material of the world it actually works with. We may not like the art we see, but for that reason may we discredit the artist? He depends on us for his inspiration. The imagination does not create *ex nihilo*. We are forced to concur with Walter Kerr: "From the cut of our clothes to the slant of our souls we are sitting to have our portraits done. They may be well done." What, above all else, do our manifold works of art tell us? Simply this: that we have lost the art of contemplation, the happy habit of dwelling with the real.

In our exclusive quest for the useful we assault the real and *abstract* from it whatever serves our purposes. We attribute no value to the thing itself but only to what we get out of it—an abstraction. We end up living in a world devoid of real things and full of abstractions. This can happen in the college world where ideas about men, magpies, and mountains can take the place of men, magpies, and mountains. It certainly does happen in the business world dominated by trade. Value is neither in the objects traded nor in the act of trading. It is in the wholly abstract, perfectly bloodless and goldless mathematical equation that $y=y$. The only worthwhile thing in the business world is this disembodied ratio. People whose lives do not revolve around the centrality of such abstract equations are regarded as unprofitable and irresponsible. People who do not fit into the equation may be abandoned; those who fit should be cultivated. Prestige and success come from keeping human relationships abstract; pride, pleasure, and contentment come from the abstractions.

But we are uneasy and restive. Why? Because though we may work with abstractions, no matter how hard we try, we cannot rest in them. It is impossible. Abstractions detach. That is their function. They enable us to think of the world without carrying the whole bloody world in our hands. They empower us to communicate with clean tidy words that may signify messy and massive world events. Industry can cope with unseen and untouched volumes of material by the abstraction of numbers. It helps to be able to sell five thousand head of cattle or a fleet of cars without bringing them into the office. Without stepping foot outside of his Royal Inn room, a man can change the world. This is a boon, indeed.

But there is a concomitant and inevitable deprivation. By his use of abstractions he loses his grip on reality. There are no cows in the word "cattle," no seven of anything in the number 7, and no mud or water or asphalt on a map. All real things are absent in their abstractions. Man cannot live on abstractions. He needs to be visibly, tangibly in touch with real things, not just their mental substitutes. I need the dog, not an empty concept (d-o-g) which we have agreed to represent by an already disembodied idea. I need God, the most real thing in the whole world, not just the names we have allowed ourselves by common consent to call him.

A balance must be kept between the raw, surd thicknesses of life and the language we use in place of them. We are out of balance now; the whole world totters. We lost our balance when we lost the art of contemplation, of communion with the Real. Our present economic and ecological crises are due to this loss; the real things left way behind uncontemplated, unloved, as the increasing use of flexible abstractions took their place. Our way of life has become so artificial we have even lost the nexus between the natural substance and the arbitrary symbol. Having forgotten the source for which the symbol stood and lost touch with the thing signified, our abstractions have blown up in our faces. Our civilizations now produce dead men, our churches pamper safe men, our drugs, while calming nerves, exhaust personalities. If we are ever to live again and venture forth humanly into deeper dimensions of being, we must insistently and troublesomely seek out proper and prolonged acts of communion with

the *concrete* upon which depends the validity and vitality of
our mental constructions.

If we cannot or will not work with the refreshingly concrete,
then all the more reason to follow the urgent promptings of
Jesus and, becoming as little children, learn to play with solid
substances again. If we are going to find God, it will not be in
pie-in-the-sky abstractions, but on the "mud-luscious" and "pud-
dle wonderful" road under our feet, and in all the lovely and
homely things along the way—the magnificent mountains and
the monotonous neighbors. Real things are not as boring as their
substitutes. They are coarse and gravity-burdened and may bind
us to the earth. But there is no loneliness or alienation in that
humble, earthy alliance.

Thus far our efforts to be pleased and ravished instead of
pushed and worked to death have been meager. The result has
been a prevalence of kitsch, a proliferation of second-rate, shallow,
insipid time killers: garish magazines with blatant pictures to
catch the eye and captions to grab the mind without engaging it;
easy-to-read digests; fancily fabricated films as thin as the celluloid
they are printed on; television that is mawkish, silly, and tor-
tuously garrulous; liturgies put together by swinging priests or
nuns for the sentimental satisfaction of love-sick people who
want to groove on one another. This is the stuff we resort to
when we do not have the time or energy to think or to pray.
But kitsch has taken over. Kerr says: "We sometimes conceive
that we live in the land of the blob: blobs of color, hoots of
sound, zoom lenses, what the comedians call 'grabbers.' Surfaces
leap at us like babies begging to be picked up; when they are
picked up, they have no weight and no conversation, only a
smile and a placid drool."

Nothing must surprise us or disturb us or involve us so profoundly that our work is interrupted.

> We are in the market—and a very limited market it
> is—for lazy delight, for incidental delight, for delight
> that need be only half attended to, for the fruits of the
> imagination made easy and unobtrusive because we have

no intention whatever of withdrawing our attention from our proper goals, from the profits to be taken from respectable employment. We do not mean to work for a while. We mean to work all of the time and let play come to us in passing, like a sandwich that is brought to the desk. [*Decline of Pleasure*, p. 136.]

Even most of the games we play require abstract counters and abstract mental processes, and so we are forced to employ, even at play, our old habits of work, computing and maneuvering in workaday fashion. These think-games foster the same kind of alertness expected of us on the job all day. They certainly do not break the work pattern of the day or refresh a tired mind. All we do is change our task. Such games belong not to the realm of pure pleasure, but to the realm of diversion. Pleasure is the intoxicating sensation of being centered, reborn, set free. Walter Kerr explains: "Pleasure is well-being itself, diversion is a temporary turning away from a lack of well-being. Pleasure is time ransomed; diversion is time passed. Pleasure changes a man; diversion changes what he is looking at, though not the quality of his looking. Whereas pleasure actively recharges, diversion keeps the battery running at an even purr."

Aristotle considered the pleasures and arts of recreation to be superior to the achievements of labor. St. Thomas Aquinas claims that no man could live without pleasure, and deprived of noble pleasures, man will seek ignoble ones. According to St. Teresa, life would not be tolerable without poetry not even in a contemplative convent.

But these ancient and saintly sages are not talking about physical recreation. We live longer today than ever before, and our bodies are stronger. It is our personalities that are diminishing. There are more kinks in our heads than in our shoulders. Our minds are flabbier than our arms and legs. Our egos are fatter than our stomachs. Half the people in America are on weight-reducing diets and various programs of physical exercise; but *moral* obesity is the problem. We are a battered and confused nation, threatened from within, dismayed by our own mental obfuscation and desuetude of will. It is our powers of belief that are grinding to a halt. The refreshment we need most urgently is not physical but intellectual. Playing cards and handball will not do the trick. What will?

More and more people are working with concepts and are, thus, willy-nilly intellectuals. Most of us, whether we like it or not, are "brain" workers, not woodsmen, farmers, or cowboys. What we must realize is that the energy we expend in intellectual work can only be renewed—and must be—by intellectual play.

> What we are digging for, and presently despairing of, is a play of the mind that will match the labor of the mind—and match it not only in kind, so that it will get at the threads that have begun to snarl, but in scale. We require an intellectual pleasure that will cause us to rejoice in our intellects; and we require an intellectual pleasure that is at least as great as the intellectual burden imposed by our work. With anything less we shall continue to slip downhill. [*Decline of Pleasure*, p. 152.]

Our minds can be refreshed and brought to something like a rebirth by only one thing: *an experience of order*.

> The order would have to be actual, not projected. It would have to be present, not rumored. It would have to be complete, not partial. It would have to be stable, not tentative. It would have to be given, not worked for. But if a man could feel himself moving, effortlessly and unerringly, through the corridors of a house in which each beam and tile, each lintel and sill, had instinctively assumed its palpably just place, in which doors opened without being touched to draw him deeper and deeper into ever more perfect and ever more central recesses, in which he knew, at the last and as he stood at its heart, that every stress of stone and argument of wood and grip of mortar and breath of air

had arrived at a pact that would hold them together forever and him in their complacent embrace, in which the whole substantial and unruffled harmony seemed to be smiling at him as though in a mirror and intimating quietly that so much buoyant proportion was only a reflection of something that he, too, possessed, it is possible that his mind would be pleased. He would not only see order and so know it for a fact. He would, for that moment, inhabit it.

It is the struggle toward an unrealized order that drains and disheartens us; only a certainty of order, whether we are participating in it or simply standing humbly before it, can mend the rent in our souls. [De-cline of Pleasure, p. 159.]

A detective novel, honestly and cleverly written, may draw us enticingly into such an experience; so may a poem or a statue; certainly music—César Franck's Symphony in D Minor is almost a sure bet! Last July on the Feast of Our Lady of Mount Carmel our community of hermits at Nova Nada, Nova Scotia, put together a marvelous bit of musical entertainment as part of our festive celebration. They came up with their own lyrics, funny and sad, pertinent and impertinent, blatant and subtle, soothing and stimulating, sacred and profane, and matched them to the music of Fiddler on the Roof. As they sang and danced and laughed and cried, our past and future, our ups and downs, our successes and failures, our fables and foibles, our tasks and dreams, our crushing disappointments and high aspirations, came marching harmoniously together into the center where Truth, clothed in splendor, erupted and enveloped us. We were surprised by joy, our spirits were uplifted, and our minds were refreshed by the clarity, certainty, and meaning of our lives. The com-munity was reborn.

T. S. Eliot is certain that "it is ultimately the function of art, in imposing a credible order upon ordinary reality, and thereby eliciting some perception of an order in reality, to bring

us to a condition of serenity, stillness, and reconciliation. . . ."
(From *Decline of Pleasure.*)

Fragmented, dispersed man is healed by order, harmony, con-
cord, and reconciliation that not only are found in art but also
are produced in man by art. There is a kind of fatigue that
even sleep cannot fix. For this we need the rejuvenating experience of order, found perhaps in a Donatello, a Terry Sulli-
van (*Desert Call* artist), or a tranquil period of prayer. "A
vision of order wakes every man up." Once awakened, the vision
we share is God's, who looked on the world he created and
beheld that it was very good.

It is God's pleasure, his delight in the goodness of the world,
that keeps it going. In fact, it is their mutual delight in the
goodness of each other that keeps love alive on the earth, reaching its deliriously delightful high point in the conscious and
intimate lovelife that goes on between God and man. The
whole incredible relationship is based on what they have in
common-goodness. God is good necessarily; the world not necessarily. God is good just because he is; but the world is good
because the eternal and creative Word continually and effectively
pronounces it so, because on each successive day of creation,
from the beginning to the end, God looks at it and says: "Good!
Very good! Terrific! Wonderful!" He looks at the way the grapes
grow in California, the way they become wine and make men
merry; and he says: "Yes, that's it; do it again!"

The world is not an intrusion on God, nor a burden, nor an
accident. The world exists by virtue of the divine applause, the
first hurrah, by means of the intimate and immediate delight
that God has in the sons of men, and in the being of everything
that is. Each thing exists because he likes it. Each one is supremely
prized by him the way a favorite rocking chair, book, or cup is
cherished by us. The world is utterly dependent on God, but
you wouldn't know it; though he is intimately present in creative
delight, he is continually self-effacing, because his delight is wholly
in the beloved creature. We who are human are not only the
objects of his delights but also the partners of his delight. But

we have shirked our creative responsibilities and our distinctive privileges. We have become so grumpy and gloomy and easily sated. How desperately we need to be pleased! We need copious supplies of mirth to get our jobs done, our destinies reached, and our vocations followed unflinchingly. St. Thomas compares community mirth to machine oil. You don't see the oil, you never notice it or think about it, but if there is no oil, if it leaks out or is used up and is not replaced, the machinery breaks down. Well, mirth is just as vitally necessary to the community as oil is to the machinery: and it is just as unpretentious.

*

Something must now be said about *the act of being pleased*. Suppose you are convinced of all that has been said so far. So you carve out a chunk of leisure time and launch into a deliberate evening of relaxation. It may prove to be psychologically unnerving and emotionally disastrous, not because of any innate reluctance on your part; you may, in fact, be too much in earnest.

Most of us make the same mistake: we tackle our pleasure with the same blunt instruments we use at work. We have brought our hammers and nails, our ledgers, graphs, and measuring tapes, and applied them to the problems of delight. We are incurably attached to habits of the mind that are good for work but bad for play. Pleasure demands a detached and playful mind. It will not yield to command but only to surrender. There is no way to govern, master, or control it. Pleasure responds to wooing and wonder, not to aggression and manipulation.

Sex is a good example. We go to meet the beloved armed to the teeth with mounds of information, multiple techniques, modern devices, determined to have an orgasm to match a *grand mal* seizure; and pleasure escapes us. No ecstasy. No exhilaration. We become so thwarted and frustrated that we go from the lover's bed to the psychiatrist's couch. Liberated though we claim to be, our anxiety over how we performed is a greater problem and harder to cure than the Victorian's anxiety over whether it should be done at all.

We cannot bulldoze our way into pleasure. Once the mind ceases to be acquisitive, pleasure will enrapture it and the delightful secrets of the universe will be revealed.

I am ready now to be more specific about the act of being pleased. But I cannot improve on Walter Kerr. Here is what he says:

> We have been searching for an intellectual act that, so far from being dispiriting, might prove restorative. It would have to be a genuine *act*, not a euphoric state: the mind would have to be attending to something, not drugged. The act would also have to be truly *intellectual*: that is to say, it would have to allow the mind to follow its own bias, which is toward knowledge and toward order, in fact toward the knowledge of order. At the same time this act would have to be free of the necessity of creating its own order: the mind's bias would have to be satisfied without exhausting effort, the threat of failure, the penalties of "work." And we now seem to be suggesting that the act should properly belong to that group of human experiences which attain their so eagerly sought objectives by approaching those objectives without evident eagerness, almost in a spirit of reserved, gentle and generous disinterest. [*Decline of Pleasure*, pp. 181–82.]

What Walter Kerr requires of us all, if we are able to be pleasured, is a playful act of the whole mind. Is there such an act? Indeed there is. It was called by the ancients (Plato and Aristotle, for instance) the act of contemplation; and it was regarded by them as the key—the only key—to perfect happiness. And all they had in mind for saying that was merely natural reasons; we have the same natural reasons plus supernatural revelation to make us overwhelmingly convinced of this truth. Ever since the ancients we have all known that the highest life is the life of contemplation (and by this I do not mean structured forms of religious life).

Our dictionary definitions, recent editions especially, have become tainted with our utilitarian bias. My own definition comes closer, I dare say, to the truth: *a long, loving, and leisurely look at the real.* If concrete things evoke from me an unselfconscious and unstudied attention, I am liable to find myself in a state of relaxed, unproductive, and intoxicating happiness.

Good art can enkindle such a state of mind. The artist is prodded in that direction by Joseph Conrad in *The Nigger of the Narcissus:* "To arrest, for the space of a breath, the hands busy about the work of the earth, and compel men entranced by the sight of distant goals to glance for a moment at the surrounding vision of form and colour, of sunshine and shadows; to make them pause for a look, for a sigh, for a smile —such is the aim, difficult and evanescent," of the artist. This is not only pertinent advice to the professional artist, but to the artist who is every man called by God into the pleasure of his good company.

Long, loving, leisurely looks take time. The real engages us and consumes our energy. If God is real, he must absorb us, each one of us, for a good part of every day. That means time must be wasted. Until I waste time prodigiously I do not take God seriously. If Christ is real, he must hold and captivate me for a lifetime; and I must dwell with him. If the persons and things around me are real, then I must take time to notice and enjoy them. If there is more real stuff in this world than I and all of us together have ever dreamed of, then I must leave lots of space in my life —space for idling until I am enchanted. Then it is high time (kairos) to follow the object of enchantment into Mystery, into the Source of all beauty and meaning, the Ultimately Real, the One, the Love beyond all other loves. This idling and following is the important, imperative, and playful part of the human adventure. Being pleased is no mindless, selfish act.

We tend to think that the contemplative act, or as we have become fond of saying today, the peak human experience, is predominantly a sensible act. The fact is that it is predominantly intellectual (superrational), with the senses playing a vigorous but supporting role. The open and receptive mind must be caught: that is the work of the senses. Once caught, it must be held and secured against distractions and lethargy: that is the function of the emotions. And so as we look out the window or in the book or at the screen or into Molly's eyes, we move from simple sensory stimulation through deep emotional commitment into a steady intuitive gaze on the truth, the blazing essence of reality.

This contemplative sequence is conspicuously noticeable in the "time" arts. Though less obvious in the "space" arts, the same pattern unfolds. A piece of sculpture may be there all at once, but we do not see it all at once. It takes time to catch us. I lived twenty-five years before I was moved deeply by a statue. I went in and out of Boston College Library for one whole year before an exquisitely carved statue of Our Lady suddenly swept me out of my daily, routine rut and I stood there motionless and breathless as I gazed in delightful astonishment at the splendid form. A red rose you have seen a hundred times can suddenly uplift you like that. One day, instead of noting it in passing, you stop and really see—you see red for the first time in your life, and you become the rose.

What is so humanly distinctive about glorying in red and exulting in a rose is that we *know* that we are being taken and we deliberately and freely surrender. And we surrender because we recognize what is happening as an unprofitable but incalculably worthwhile experience. But it is, and this is important, as we shall see at the end of this chapter—knowledge "on the wing," rather than any kind of self-scrutiny. It is under the steady gaze of the intellect that the many scattered and isolated things that have tingled the flesh, quickened the blood, and fired the imagination now become One Thing that enthralls the mind, which blinks once, stands back, and sees the balance. "In this decisive act of perceiving an order among parts, a harmony in differences, beginnings in ends and ends in beginnings, urgency is resolved and passion spent," Walter Kerr tells us.

The catharsis experienced at this point is not the emotional splurge and purge that spills over a fervid rally, a football game,

or a pentecostal meeting. The cathartic satisfaction occurs in the
reconciling powers of the mind. It is an intellectual not an in-
testinal purgation. How much more appropriately beautiful and
enduringly fruitful our eucharistic celebrations would be if this
truth were realized. Preposterous paroxysms and caricatures of
liturgy could then be eliminated once and for all. I, for one,
would appreciate anything that would reduce the ridiculous situa-
tions I run into "on the road." When I arrived at one retreat house
and saw the glorious chapel, I could hardly wait to celebrate Mass
there. Well, I was deprived of that awesome and prayerful privilege. The staff, "an exciting and sensitive team"—hustled me and
the bewildered group of retreatants into a dingy back room where
we offered the holy and august sacrifice, the most solemn rites of
the Roman Catholic Church, on an ironing board. Devilishly
cute! On another occasion I took the place of a priest who
regularly offered Mass for his "floating parish." As Father would
have said, it was a "blast." At the kiss of peace the schoolroom
rocked and reverberated with stentorian demonstrations of jubilant
and boisterous affection; the corybantic tide swelled, worshipers
driven by their own blissful exuberance ended up in the school-
yard where the kissing, hugging, and yelling increased. I stood at
the altar—alone, amused, and appalled. They never came back!

A genuine contemplative catharsis involves a play of the mind,
including the subconscious areas, that is equivalent to the athlete's
sport.

> The contemplative, similarly, exposes himself to ar-
> bitrary challenges—to sensations that lure without prom-
> ising immediate relief, to emotional disturbances that
> may even be painful—so that the ripple of his nerve ends
> and the ground swell of his emotions may be brought to
> the poised perfection of a majestic whitecap, known in
> its mass and its balance and its shivering harmony during
> the long moment of its climactic suspension, exercised
> and then exorcised by a perceiving intelligence. Parting
> company with the athlete, the contemplative does not
> bestir himself physically. But he has submitted more of

the whole man to the joyous whipcracking of the intellect: he has brought the senses and the emotions dancing into the ring, for the specific purpose of letting his mind draw a ring around them.

His mood is playful, though the things to be played over include the whole of the world in which he normally works. His activity is ultimately and essentially intellectual, though all sorts of passions are made to dance to the mind's tune. [*Decline of Pleasure,* pp. 201–02.]

It is the *lover* (in the deep robust sense of the word), not the *thinker,* who really knows. The thinker begins with the tree, the flower, the rabbit, and goes on an intellectual romp through the world riding high on universals. The lover wants to play, to be like a child and come home again. But how shall an adult, after so many years in the logical stratosphere, come home?

He must stop thinking. Am I contradicting myself? Is it absurd for me to insist on the mindfulness of contemplation and almost in the same breath say that if you are going to contemplate you must give up thinking? Am I on to a new wrinkle, a fad? Hardly. No-thinking has been the crucial guideline of the oldest spiritual tradition of mankind. And the no-ness of this Hindu tradition became progressively emphasized in Buddhism, and especially in Zen. But it is not exclusively an oriental insight. It was Aristotle who noticed that the contemplative power, the power that produces pleasure, "seems to become stronger when the reasoning power is relaxed." Since what we are after is a relaxation of mental powers rather than a repudiation, *vertical thinking,* as the Jesuit author Father William Johnston suggests, might be a better term than *no-thinking.* Vertical thinking, a simple intuition of truth, does not embroil us in the logical and laborious procedure of discursive knowledge. If it did, it would rule out play. The lover, like the child, forfeits the worldwide analogical tour of *being* in favor of savoring single, concrete things: one dog named Zorba, one old hat, one brand-new pair of boots, one human face.

After all, strictly speaking, there is no isolated object. If we really learn how to see, we will enjoy a pure intuition born of love and thus behold the manifold in the one. By focusing prayer-fully on one hazelnut Juliana of Norwich came to perceive the meaning of herself, her neighbors, the universe, and God. We do not need multiple and varied experiences to free us from our parochial and conventional viewpoint; we need one unselfing, insightful experience of what Gerard Manley Hopkins calls "the dearest freshness deep down things." Inscape and landscape con-verge. One and one hundred are the same distance from infinity. Emmanuel Chapman, paraphrasing St. Augustine, defines the contemplative act that we have been analyzing: "Intuitive knowl-ledge" is an experience in which "the mind, without any ef-fort of abstraction, is irradiated by an intelligible light which is delightfully apprehended."

This playful, openhearted dwelling with the real is no childish, empty-headed regression. We do not rub out knowledge already acquired or obliterate abstractions for the sake of teapots and turtles. It just happens that when we come back home to rest in the simple single things that give birth to our big, wide, wonderful mental world, our abstractions rest there, too. There is no violent abrogation or repression whatsoever. As we are drawn by love through the form we feel and the eyes we see into the inner sanctum of this singular rabbit, we are in touch, finally, with something we have signified and symbolized a thousand times in books, pictures, and films: signified but never touched. Now in holy, embodied communion something private and singular and unique is touched, and revealed as such in the touching.

This kind of communion is so holy and so deep it eludes the grasp of verbalization. The rabbit, as such, remains incommuni-cable. That is why I can, given half a chance, discourse on girls, but not on Patty whom I love. Then I begin to twitter and stutter effervescently, and my friends may say, "What does he see in her?" See is the right word, because lovers know by seeing, not by ab-stracting. It's a vision no detached observer or listener can share. But this knowledge of the heart is more certain and more valuable than the most brilliant brainstorms of ratiocination. Discursive thought is just one way, albeit a vastly important one, of searching out the truth. There are other less circuitous and laborious ways. So many truths, perhaps the ultimate truths, are disclosed only to the playful mind.

> It was the dog, the cat and the dolphin, working out their own destinies, that taught me how to play. "In the behaviour of a cat, a dog, a dolphin," writes Teilhard [de Chardin], "there is such suppleness, such unexpectedness, such exuberance of life and curiosity! . . . It takes interest, it flutters, it plays. . . . Around it an *aura* of freedom begins to float, a glimmer of personality. . . ." If I sometimes find it easier to *play* when there is a dog or a cat around, it is no doubt because I am entertaining, and being entertained by, the companion who discovered playfulness and left it to me as a legacy —a legacy I have neglected and of which I need to be reminded. [*Decline of Pleasure*, p. 220.]

The playful activation of the superrational powers of the mind engenders in us the best of all ways of knowing: intuition, which does not inform us about things but puts us in immediate *contact* with things, ultimately, in mystical knowledge, with everything all at once; and at that point an unspeakably wonderful thing happens: *at-one-ment*, or the coincidence of opposites.

An earlier chapter tried to show how the freedom to love is lost in the compulsion to possess. Delightful serendipities come and go. We cannot force them or guarantee them. If we bide our time, the sun will come out again, the deer will appear on the road, maybe even a century plant will bloom. We cannot create, at will, what re-creates us. We have the capacity to be pleased. The capacity will never become a habitually honed instrument of ecstasy unless we manage to get our grasping hands out of the way.

The contemplative is easily pleased and deeply nourished precisely because he comes to the other empty-handed. It is hard for God or Beethoven to put anything into a closed fist. A cluttered mind or a crowded heart impedes the art of contemplation and therefore precludes any pleasurable consequences. That is why St. John of the Cross is so pitilessly hard on appetites. They fritter away our capacity for ecstasy. Everytime we pander to these frivolous intruders, possibilities of real pleasure dwindle. Just when the waiter comes with champagne, our glasses are full of Kool-Aid.

Self-interest can spoil a contemplative event. As Victor Frankl points out, people who try too hard and too directly to be happy end up in his office. That "pursuit of happiness" phrase in the Declaration of Independence of the United States is a misleading one. It is not what the founding fathers originally had in mind. They wanted to guarantee the pursuit of private property. A controversy arose. "Pursuit of happiness" was felt to be an innocuous enough compromise. It was unfortunate. It encouraged a materialistic hedonism.

But being overly interested in another can also interrupt the contemplative act. If you go to your husband's lecture or his concert and are too much concerned about him, it may turn out to be a religious experience for everyone else; but certainly not for you. I recall sitting behind the wife of the oboe soloist at a performance by the Boston Pops. Although the man played brilliantly and even flawlessly, his wife was a nervous wreck, twisting and turning in her chair and wringing her hands continuously. She ruined not only her own enjoyment but mine, too, and that of everyone else around her. Pure delight fills the irresistible space of pure disinterest. Most of us hardly ever hear or see or feel the world because our minds are so worried about what to think of it. The world we detach ourselves from is the only world we will come to enjoy.

We tend to devour whatever promises pleasure and thus blow the delicate opportunities. We pounce on a good thing and consume it: but that does not produce happiness. Happiness is the fruit of contemplation. Two lively concomitant activities constitute the act of contemplation: intuition of the truth and vital union with the good. This integral act issues, of course, in love, which is the main thing. But you cannot love what you do not know. If our lives are loveless, it does not necessarily mean that we are heartless. We may be sightless. Sinful man keeps steeling his will when he should be sharpening his mind. He should be doing both really, since the human adventure is a gradual and gracious enlargement of the mind. But I suspect we blame our bad wills too much and our sluggish minds not enough. How many times have you resolved, with all the goodwill in the world, never again to be unkind to a friend or fellow worker? Two hours later you meet him and he gives you that same old stupid look. So you pummel him. What happened? Well, your beating was executed with as much goodwill as your resolution. But you were caught off guard and lost your perspective, your insight. You forgot who he was: a living image and likeness of God, a temple of the Holy Spirit, another Christ, one for whom Jesus died. In the absence of this knowledge of things as they really are, you behaved abominably. The cause of your disreputable behavior was not bad will but fuzzy thinking. That is why St. Thomas Aquinas said that in one sense all sin was an intellectual mistake. All those "apparent" goods that suck us into subhuman levels of acting do so by means of an intellectual trick, a hallucination.

So there is no contemplative life and, consequently, no happiness without intuition and vital union. Consuming the loaf of bread is vital union; perceiving the beautiful wheatness of bread is intuition. Eating a peach is vital union; relishing the roundness and fuzziness of a peach is intuition. Joining a group is vital union; seeing the connections and knowing why is intuition. Taking a girl to bed is vital union; a perceptive appreciation of who she is is intuition. Receiving the consecrated host is vital union; knowing that it is Christ, son of the living God, is intuition.

All the unhappy individuals and communities I know, secular or religious, are unhappy because they are uncontemplative; and they are unfruitful for the same reason. They are uncontemplative because one of these essential ingredients, intuition or vital union, suffers a serious diminution or is eclipsed. In most cases the collapse of contemplative life is due to a failure of intuition. In fact, the Greeks were so impressed with the function of intuition that they mistakenly designated it, and it alone, as contemplation. Lots of people, failing to recognize, since the coming of Christ, the new incarnational element that now invests all authentic forms of contemplation, perpetuate this fallacy. Nevertheless, intuition is still of paramount importance.

The present chaotic state of family life followed upon the disintegration of intuitive life. The breakdown of marital life and spousal love is due in most cases to a gradual deadening of the intuitive life of marriage partners. If love is threatened, the typical solution is to multiply the activities, talk more, do many more things together, enjoy the coital act more frequently—all forms of vital union—but the marriage peters out anyway and the love turns to dust and ashes. Why? Ordinarily because of a lack of intuition, a failure to understand the problem. What happens is this: When two lovers decide that they belong to each other and therefore stop looking for each other, the mysterious other hidden behind the masks and symbols we use for introductions and easy access to superficial dimensions of being, then the love is doomed. Love begins to disintegrate when they stop taking long loving looks at one another, cease to discern deeper levels of personality, give up their solitude and silence, their leisure and privacy for the sake of euphoric togetherness. Once they surface and do not return to the deep, still caverns of the intuitive life, frenzied forays into vital union will not help. Dashed hopes, frustrations, and bitterness are inevitable.

Another example. Suppose I am "on the road." I am scheduled for Milwaukee where I have not been in years. Some particularly good friends decide to have a party for the occasion. They spend lots of time preparing: they write our mutual friends; they remember my favorite food and prepare it fastidiously; the margaritas are in the refrigerator; carefully selected music is playing in the background; the table is set impeccably with an exquisite tablecloth, elegant china, beautiful flowers and candles. What a magnificent setting created out of such thoughtful love! I arrive. The trouble is that I have not eaten in a couple of days. So I am driven by appetite, longing for vital union with food. A driven man is not a free man. He wants to consume and not contemplate. I am so famished and so attracted by food—not any particular kind of food, it does not matter—that I do not even notice the specially good things and the generous love behind them. I ignore my friends, disregard the table and the music, fail to distinguish the different kinds of food, and pay no heed to the conversation. All I do is consume food and thereby satisfy my appetite. That kind of vital union was achieved. But because I did not contemplate, or more correctly, because I was not intuitive, I missed what was, by far, the most important dimensions of this feast, the most meaningful gifts of love.

Except in heaven and in some mystical foretastes of heaven we cannot have everything all at once. It was not possible for me at that Milwaukee feast to enjoy such unmitigated vital union with the "good" (food) and intuit the "true" and the "beautiful" at the same time. The only way I could know how *good* the food was was to eat it. The only way I could know how *beautiful* it all was and the *true* meaning behind it was to leave the food alone.

We are unable to live by bread alone because we have larger appetites. Man has, for instance, "an appetite for the untouched, for the virginal if you will, for that primary, natural, unmolested radiance in the presence of which his aggressive will is quieted and only his mind is pleased. This is an appetite satisfied by admiration alone. The goodness of the object is held in abeyance while the glory of the subject is feasted upon." (*Decline of Pleasure*) In other words, only a man who has eradicated lust and quelled all forms of craving can contemplate a pretty girl. Such a pure form of girl-watching involves both elements of the contemplative act: intuition and vital union. There is no possession, no dominion, no commingling of the flesh. But what the contemplative intuits he loves, and love binds him forever to that girl. But at a price: All that was seductively good about her, all that he might have had, he let go. Nor does he strain to recall the specific outlines of that experience, so that he leaves the scene as he came in—empty-handed. There is no way to reproduce the contemplative act in the same form or to recapture its vivifying effects. All such perfervid attempts fracture a man's spirit and leave him a shambles. That is why Catholic Pentecostalism is so uncontemplative and why so many have lost their balance as a result of it.

How do we resist the irrespressible urge to use, to exploit, to be paid? Walter Kerr suggests, rightly I am sure, that we need vice-tight patterns that become absolute barriers against profit-taking. The first thing to do is slam the door on the encroachments of the workaday world; then devise some hilarious activities, the more preposterous and arbitrary, the better, and bestow some token prizes, charming but useless.

Let me say, finally, pleasure is free but not frivolous. It has a value of its own, and it comes from the Other. All our small pleasures are little bits and pieces of the one delight we all seek, consciously or unconsciously, most of all: *the pleasure of God's company*.

*

Now we are in a better position to understand how Jeremy Bentham, the utilitarian and the worker, could establish his system on the principle of pleasure. The practice of his philosophy is, in fact, the prostitution of pleasure. The utilitarian determination to get pleasure out of God and heighten the pleasure and fasten it down by measuring it is the knife in the back of contemporary religion.

Much of today's preoccupation with altered states of consciousness has far more to do with the isolated exaltation of man than with the adoration of God. One of the interesting things that electroencephalographology has demonstrated is that the human brain puts out at least four kinds of electrical currents, referred to by researchers as alpha, beta, delta, and theta waves. Theta waves are the exciting ones. Technicians believe that these are the waves that account for the visions of the great mystics and for the focused attention of people who have practiced meditation for a long time. As a result of this research, the investigators are convinced that what took the saintly ascetic three years to accomplish can now be attained in three weeks. Many people have been lured away by this simple device from the arduous following of Christ. Consequently pseudomystics abound. Letting technique dominate religious experience is comparable to attributing an uproariously happy marriage of twenty-five years to sexual technique. Anyone who is serious about man or God, moksha or satori, will not see in that wavy line any evidence for what or whom he is passionately seeking. So far in human history the result of technique has been, not a heightening, but rather a narrowing and flattening of human experience. Eric Gill's poignant cry still rings in the air. "Good Lord, the thing was a mystery and we tried to measure it." (*Decline of Pleasure.*)

The narcissist is a miserable contemplative. He contemplates himself (a kind of mystical masturbation). And that is what makes him miserable. It is impossible to enjoy yourself while you contemplate yourself. In other words, the enjoyment and the contemplation of our inner activities are incompatible. When you see a sunset, you enjoy the act of seeing and contemplate the sunset. When you touch a perfect body, you enjoy the feeling and contemplate the body. Later on if you analyze the sense of touch or scrutinize your feeling, you are then contemplating the feeling and enjoying the thought. In the wake of your beloved's death you contemplate the death and enjoy the grief. If you grieve too long, your friends begin to worry and so they contemplate your loneliness and enjoy their anxiety.

If you look at your faith, you stop believing at that moment; if you look at your love, you stop loving; if you look at your hope, you stop hoping. You interrupt these God-centered acts by turning around to look at them. Once you squint back to see how you are contemplating, you cease to contemplate—or you change the object of your contemplation. The surest way to spoil a meal or an encounter is to start examining your satisfaction. All introspection is to some degree short-circuited: we try to look inside ourselves to see what is going on, but the moment we look it stops. Instead we find mental images and physical sensations. C. S. Lewis writes about all this in *Surprised by Joy*. "The great error," he says, "is to mistake this mere sediment or track or by-

product for the activities themselves." Not that these activities, before we stopped them, were unconscious. Lewis says that we need
more than the twofold division into conscious and unconscious.
We need a threefold division: the unconscious, the enjoyed, and
the contemplated.

Most contemplative efforts in our narcissistic age are futile attempts to contemplate the enjoyed. We are determined to capture
joy, so we swallow pills, take injections, consume alcohol, exploit
others, go on trips, reveal our naked bodies, and bare our souls;
we prowl around the sanctuary of our psyches looking for high experiences; and all that we find is either an image or a quiver in the
diaphragm, "a mental track left by the passage of joy, and not the
wave but the wave's imprint on the sand."

RELIGIOUS EXPERIENCE

Chapter 5 – The Heart of Religion

We have explained the human adventure thus far in terms of life humanly experienced. We have used words such as "religious" and "mystical" and "Christian" as qualifying words but did not stop to examine them as important and distinguishable entities. Our concentration has centered on the word "experience" because experience is the key to a full life. Only the experienced man knows life because he knows what it feels like: the sand, the rain, the grass, and the wind; the body of a dog, a cat, a man, or a woman; working hands and dancing feet; the agony and ecstasy of death and rebirth; the many different kinds of human hate and love; and the touch of God.

There is a lot of religious, mystical, and Christian talk going on today without an underlying experience to validate the plethora of words. We bury ourselves under an avalanche of ideas, problems, projects, and programs, a million meanings and purposes—with no experience—and so we suffer and die without ever having lived. We skim along the surface of life with information enough to busy the mind forever and make a derivative existence seem plausible. But without firsthand experience we do not really know and we do not really live.

Observation, conceptualization, conversation, or pedantic dithering cannot take the place of direct and experiential awareness. Subsequent reflection and integration can and often do enlarge and enrich the experience; and the experience can be partially shared by careful articulation. But the heart of the experience is being in a predominantly conscious love relationship with the Other. Almost any kind of a relationship is better than none; man cannot survive in a vacuum or in the solipsistic wastelands of the isolated ego.

Even as I write this, I feel trapped by my own words—words that might take the place of action. Our words are more humanistic and existential than ever before. They are crisp and fresh—and maybe fraudulent. I think of all the new books about sea gulls and pelicans and rabbits and lions, and I wonder if we will allow these marvelous creatures to take our place in the arena of life as we look on and applaud. I see bright and wordy posters and banners in our institutions all over the country, and they frequently emphasize dancing; but I never see any dancing. The young Marx and Engels lambasted ideologists who substituted the idealistic category of *dancing* for the frank sensuality of the can-can:

> The reverend parson speaks here neither of the *can-can* nor of the *polka*, but of dancing in general, of the category, Dancing, which is not performed anywhere except in his critical cranium. If he saw a single dance at the Chaumière in Paris his Christian German soul would be outraged by the boldness, the frankness, the graceful petulance and the music of that most sensual movement. [Joseph Tamney, "Religion as the Art of Suicide," in *Listening*, Vol. 3 No. 2, Spring 1968.]

There is the rub—and the trap set for us all!

Read the opening paragraph of St. John's Epistle (I John 1:1–4):

> That which was from the beginning, which we have heard, which we have seen with our eyes, which we have looked upon and touched with our hands, concerning the word of life—the life was made manifest, and we saw it, and testify to it, and we proclaim to you the eternal life which was with the Father and was made manifest to us—that which we have seen and heard we

proclaim also to you, so that you may have fellowship with us; and our fellowship is with the Father and with his Son Jesus Christ. And these things we write you that you may rejoice, and our joy may be full.

That is experience. It is the stuff of life and the paramount point of Christianity.

Experience is fed by both conscious and unconscious areas of the psyche. What lies on the dark side of the boundary of consciousness can at times be apprehended as a significant part of an experience. And we know that there is a persistent drive, often repressed or sublimated, to extend the boundaries and transcend the limits of ordinary consciousness. The many recent studies on the "peak human experience" by Abraham Maslow, for instance, elucidate this point quite accurately and impressively. So does Roberto Assagioli's *Psychosynthesis*—in a more commonly applicable way. And so—far more than St. Thomas and recent forms of Scholasticism—do the more ancient writings of the Fathers of the Church.

The findings of modern psychology, particularly Jungian psychology and depth analysis, are a great help because they bear out the deepest experiences of the mystics. The ancient Fathers, Clement, Origen, and Gregory of Nyssa, for instance, and the outstanding modern psychologists agree that knowledge is not the result of mere reasoning but the outcome of our union with all being, finite and infinite. On this point both the ancients and the moderns disagree with Scholasticism's confinement of knowledge to the conscious mind and its repudiation of the Christian gnosis of the Fathers and the holistic insight of contemporary Christian humanists.

Man is far more than his conscious mind. If man had not activated his *whole* mind—his whole manhood, including *sub* and *super* rational powers, the demonic and angelic realms of his being—and developed in himself appropriate, subjective dispositions, there would have been no revelation. God would have come crashing into the human world with no one there to receive him.

God does not act, does not reveal himself, in a vacuum. He

needs man as a conscious and willing medium of his revelation. The mystic arrives at his loving awareness of God, the unitive state, by an arduous psychological and spiritual process, the mystic way, involving transformation of character and altered consciousness. St. John of the Cross and C. G. Jung agree that the path of mystical unfoldment and the process of individuation, which are similar experiences, demand a heroic effort on the part of him who is following the pilgrim path toward self-realization. Divine revelation depends on self-realization. That is obvious, since revelation is the enunciation of truth as seen by the illumined consciousness.

Discursive reasoning, merely one, though important, function of the mind, needs to detach and dissect the real into mentally manageable abstractions for the sake of mapping and discussing the pilgrimage into the Absolute, the inner journey of everyman. But it is only a superrational kind of action that undertakes the whole venture, and a faithful adherence to the promptings of the Holy Spirit that completes it. It is of this intuitive knowledge that John Ruysbroeck, the Flemish contemplative, in some ways the most wonderful of the mystics, speaks when he says: "What we are, that we behold, and what we behold, that we are. Our thought, our life and our being are uplifted in simplicity and are made one with truth." (*The Adornment of the Spiritual Marriage.*)

If man had not already known something of God, there would have been no faith. Faith simply clarified what man already knew dimly through his natural kinship with God. The object of faith may be defined as that which is rationally but not empirically certain. It is rationally certain because it is the only total picture that co-ordinates all the facts in a satisfying way; it is not empirically certain, because it involves a reality that cannot be verified by direct observation. It is this concept of faith that Paul seeks to convey to the Hebrews when he writes: "Faith gives substance to our hopes, and makes us certain of realities we do not see" (Heb. 11:1). And it underlies Paul's pugnacious words when he declares: "Their unbelieving minds are so blinded by the god of this passing age, that the Gospel of the glory of Christ, who is the very image of God, cannot dawn upon them and bring them light" (II Cor. 4:4). If you limit knowledge to the conscious and define faith as an intellectual assent to something that we know nothing about whatsoever, then you are bound to consign the higher consciousness of the mystics to museum items of esoteric interest but of no normative or educational value to the Church or common man.

It is only if man activates both the conscious and the unconscious areas of his whole mind that he is able to live by love and thus transcend the paraphernalia of the Church, all religiosity, and become a dynamic person vitalized by the center of the Church, the heart of religion. Let me affirm the importance and indispensable nature of the context, the "letter" of religiousness that is religion. But this letter belongs to me. I do not belong to it. It helps me to belong to God. No person is religious in a vacuum. He becomes religious by participating in one or other of the historical traditions. Yet each man's participation is his own. And religious truth or falsity lies in that participation, rather than having been determined in advance by the institutional pattern. Belonging, ultimately, to a religion instead of God is an inexcusable form of enslavement. But a haughty rejection of religion is an equally binding capitulation. The crucial question is not which religion is *true*, but whether or not you and I are praying out of our own *inner* truth. A religion, Christianity, for instance, is not true absolutely, impersonally, statically; rather, it can *become* true, if and insofar as you or I appropriate it to ourselves and interiorize it, live it out from day to day. A religion becomes true as we take it off the shelf and personalize it, in dynamic actual existence.

We have learned from the excellent studies of Professor Wilfred Cantwell Smith that the very concept of "religion" has evolved in the Western world and in fact *reified:* that is, mentally we have made religion into a *thing*. What used to be the processive and progressive experience of a people has become a circumscribed entity. Instead of flowing with the water's current, we have crawled out of the stream, sat on the bank, and begun to study the stream.

No word in either Latin or Greek corresponds exactly to our

English usage of "religion." And the languages of the ancient civilizations of India, China, Japan, Iran, Egypt, the Tigris-Euphrates Valley, and the Aztec peoples contained no term for "religion" at all. The Hindus, for example, developed religious ideals and practices in richer profusion earlier than any other people. But the Hindus' religiousness remained integrated and coterminus with their very existence and was not relegated to a distinct and isolated segment of their life called religion. There were Hindus, but no Hinduism. They were able to be religious without reifying.

Nor was there a Buddhist religion in India; but there was a Buddhist community. And in China the result of Buddhist missionary activity was not an organization, but a tradition. Classical Hebrew has no word signifying "religion," and the Old Testament is innocent of the term. The New Testament speaks not of religion but of *faith*. Scripture gives no evidence that the early Christians were conscious of being involved in a new religion. C. S. Lewis has pointed out how hard it is to imagine the word on the lips of Jesus Christ himself!

If we turn to Taoism we find an instance where the argument against use of such a concept needs to be made most strongly. Lao-tzu and Chuang-tzu preached that reality, Tao, is not a neat and ordered system nor a code of rules, but a process: dynamic, vital, and ebullient. The two oriental giants must have turned in their graves when the freedom they proclaimed for man reified! No modern thinker has debunked religious rigidity with anything like their vigor and verve, their grace and wit, their pith and brilliance. If their Tao is valid, then Taoism is false. According to Lao-tzu: "I do not know its name. If I am forced to give it a name, I call it Tao, and I name it as supreme. Supreme means going on; going on means going far. . . ." (*Way of Life*.)

For the devout Jew, revelation proclaims not Judaism but justice, and man's proper response is an ultimate loyalty not to a system but to a community and to the Most High God. Many Jewish scholars refuse to reduce Judaism to a religion, insisting that such a reduction is a betrayal of its true nature.

Similarly, in the *Bhagavad-Gita,* when Krishna, who has been disguised as Arjuna's charioteer, has led Arjuna to a point where he is capable of responding to a divine revelation, he does not reveal Hinduism but himself, a personal God: "God dwells in the heart of all beings, Arjuna: thy God dwells in thy heart. . . . Give thy mind to me, and give me thy heart, and thy sacrifice, and thy adoration. This is my Word of promise: thou shalt in truth come to me, for thou art dear to me."

It is as Christians' faith in God has weakened that they have busied themselves with Christianity, and as their personal relationship with Christ has waned that they have turned to religion. So many Christians today speak about believing in Christianity rather than believing in Christ himself and God his Father. They preach Christianity instead of the good news of Christ Jesus and practice Christianity instead of love. They talk about being saved by Christianity rather than by the bloody anguish and self-sacrificing love of Jesus the Galilean.

It is only since the Enlightenment two centuries ago that we have begun to reify the fluid dynamism of religiousness into religions: intellectualist systems, patterns of doctrine, so that they could be labeled Taoism or Christianity or Hinduism or Judaism.

This tendency to reify and turn a dynamic flow of religiousness into a thing has impelled us toward such gross and complicated forms of religiosity that what began as a subtle and transparent means of binding man to God (the institution, for instance) came to be an impediment. Certainly we cannot live without structure or institutional means; what we have got to do is constantly refine and reform such means so they do not become the end.

It is high time we turned strongly and unstintingly against the *bureaucracy,* not the *institution.* A bureaucracy is a hierarchical structure having considerable power and low circulation, whereas an institution is characterized as a pattern of culture traits specialized to the shaping and distribution of particular values. Remaining in the Roman Catholic Church today despite the institutional mess should be a free and deliberate choice. My reason for this is that the hierarchical institutions of the Roman Catholic Church, with all their decadence, their corruption and confusion, do in fact link me and all the rest of us to areas of Christian truth beyond our own particular experience and ultimately to truths beyond any experience.

The Church exists for *prayer*—to unite men to God, in Christ, and unite them as intimately as possible, in this life, here and now. It is prayer that penetrates reality and discerns the spiritual truth that is the veritable deposit of faith.

Contemplative insight is the foundation and source of Christian doctrine. The doctrine perpetuates the insight and saves the new Christian from beginning from scratch. This was affirmed by the English mystic Augustine Baker when he wrote in *Holy Wisdom:*

> The first knowledge of our mysteries of Christian religion came in and by contemplations . . . to which God called the apostles, doctors and other principal members and beginners of the Church and to them in the said contemplations revealed the said mysteries, and by them hath communicated and imparted the same to other Christians who took it by tradition from those contemplators who *saw and felt* the truth of those mysteries.

This contemplative insight is not a product of human industry or genius, although human preparation and participation are unskippable steps toward the center where the insight occurs, where the gift is received—the *mystical experience.* The immediate experience of God may come in many ways and under many symbolic disguises. It may be steady or fleeting, dim or intense, but insofar as it is direct and intuitive, it is always a mystical experience. A firsthand experience of God, the Absolute Reality, and a life controlled by the love that that experience awakens: this is what unites all mystics, Christian and non-Christian alike; therefore, unity of the human world depends upon the growing number of mystics.

This concept of mysticism relieves us from narrow and exclusive conceptions, since God's demand on the human person, his confrontation with man—this man, personal, unique, unrepeatable—is a universal truth experienced by different people in many different ways and degrees. This statement seems to cover all mystics, from the impersonal ecstasy of Plotinus with his longing after the one to the Christocentric passion of St. Bernard or Richard Rolle, from the eucharistic mysticism of St. Thomas or Catherine of Genoa to the inner light of the Quaker saints. It is part of the business of organized religion to arouse and feed this Godward thirst and so to make us more human, more adventurous, more alive.

This God-centered vitality makes a man not only alive to God but alive to God's world, delicately and intelligently in tune with what goes on there. This worldly grounded theology, so characteristic of religion in the Western world, is due to the predominance of the incarnational principle, namely, that man becomes at his full development a creative personality, a cocreator with God. The promise made in the first chapter of Acts is literally fulfilled in man: his living contemplation, his prayer in the Spirit, produces power, power on earth.

As a consequence of this unfolding principle, all of our genuine mystics turn out to be earthy mystics, active practical men, not content with self-loss in peace and the blessedness of eternity. For the earthy mystic, union with God means self-giving to the purposes of divine energy and love in the world. And so, Paul, Bernard, Francis, Joan of Arc, John Wesley, Elizabeth Fry, and the Curé of Ars lived lives of immense apostolic power and agreed with Ruysbroeck's saying that the final stage of the mystic is not ecstatic self-loss in the Godhead but something at once more difficult and divine—"a wide-spreading love toward all in common." This is what Baron von Hügel calls inclusive mysticism, which precludes pantheistic tendencies and sloppy claims to be in tune with the infinite.

We must not stop short of the *life of the spirit*. That's what religion is all about, as distinct from the religiosity and pietisms of so many of the do-gooders, talkers, and faddists of today.

There is a word recurrent in the Psalms and the liturgy that sums up the distinctive wisdom of genuine religiousness: *cor*, heart. That is why a deep devotion to the Sacred Heart has a robust theological character to it. The heart of Jesus is his spirit, not his physiological blood pump, which is merely the symbol. This *hearty* devotion, therefore, is directed to a *human* spirit in its most intimate union with the Divine Superspirit. "I am the way, the truth, and the life": the *heart of religion*.

*

Unless we do our thinking about God and the world from this creative and Christic center of the universe, our theology is bound to become esoteric, enthroned in isolated splendor in a sacred and sealed-off compartment of its own, untouched by the hurly-burly of life in the world. This is precisely what has happened, bringing with it the inevitable consequence: an emasculated theology, singularly unprayerful and unworldly, woefully unable to feed a feeble and floundering people on the march through history toward the Kingdom of God, that is, toward the divinely human world of Christ-men building the earth on the Gospel principles of love.

Theological reflection is an integral part of, but no more than, the *conceptual embodiment* of religious experience. The theology of God must not be so loud and labial that the Word himself is muffled. If theology is not a prayerful reflection on God whom the theologian has experienced, then what he offers is no more than a reformulation, more fashionable than ever perhaps, of old theological propositions. It is hard to imagine such dull, detached doctrine ever becoming the foundation or motivation for robust and adventurous ascetical endeavors or mystical enjoyments. Experience must be restored to its rightful place in theology; doctrinal truth and a life of prayer must be wedded again. Theology begins with experience, and experience reflected upon produces theology, which in turn interprets and guides experience.

The religious experience that theology expresses and in turn assists must not be confined to peak religious experiences, such as sudden conversions or dramatic forms of ecstasy. It seems to me that people who claim they never have anything like a religious experience are unduly restricting the notion of religious experience. Reflection is an integral part of the experience. Important dimensions of existence would be lost without it. Transcendence, for instance, lies within the boundaries of a more encompassing experience. And this expansion of the limits of consciousness occurs through a fresh look at everyday experience. Theology can foster the enjoyment of an expanding consciousness by alerting men to what Peter Berger calls signals of transcendence in everyday experience, and by challenging contemporary assumptions and attitudes, and whatever else might make it difficult for man to be present to himself, to others, and to God.

By keeping vital religious traditions alive and communicating them effectively, theology can help man break through the barriers that temporally and spatially confine him. The theologian himself must be a man of prayer, awesomely steeped in mystery; otherwise he will convey the absence of God instead of his presence.

To be with God is the goal of all human striving. Love is what unites. So the perfection of love is the essence of the Christian life, of human existence. Not to "groove" on God, not even to possess him, but to be with him so totally that you, in a sense, become him: that is the end of all truly human aspirations. To make experience, in a solipsistic sense, the focal aim of one's quest is inevitably self-frustrating. Aliveness, an overflowing vitality, does involve an appropriate self-awareness, but this genuine kind of self-consciousness is a by-product of an unselfconscious relatedness to what is not ourselves. So the possibilities of religious experience are heightened by a self-oblivious dedication to the glory of God, the well-being of man, and harmony in the universe.

A theology divorced from experience, a dehydrated tradition deprived of "living water," the mystical element, is bound to express itself in an effete and flaccid liturgy. Despite all our dabbling in liturgical reform, despite the guitars and folk singing, the colloquial language and comradely informality, our forms of worship seem, for the most part, indecorous and decadent.

I recently received a letter from a nun whose comments match those I get from all kinds of people all over the country:

> I surely miss Mass that is both simple and solemn, reverent and right. I get a little weary of (or, worse yet, amused at) these rather emotional Masses where the sweet spirit of Gee-zuz flutters into our dark, deep innermost souls, drenching us with true light and uniting us to hand-clutching, everlasting friendships (whether or not we even so much as know each others' names, for crying out loud). Ah, well. It's the in-thing, and I suppose people really do profit from these "happenings." But what can ever improve upon the simple, plain little group, with Father going straight through the rubrics *sans* embellishments, no scintillating guitars vibrating in the shadows.

I regret to say that Sister's experience does not conflict with much of my own observation of worship when I am "on the road": liturgical performances that are permeated with frenetic banter, eupeptic gesticulations, and jolly hymnody. It's all so very chummy, groovy, and planned. Until we can throw away the pile of program notes and dispense with the program director explaining everything and stoking people from the pulpit, liturgy will not be revived.

We suffer from what C. S. Lewis described over ten years ago as "liturgical fidget" with our need for "incessant brightenings, lightenings, lengthenings, abridgements, simplifications, and complications of the service . . . [which] can have only an entertainment value." "The perfect church service," he continues in his *Letters to Malcom: Chiefly on Prayer*, "would be one we were almost unaware of; our attention would have been on God. But every novelty prevents this. It fixes our attention on the service itself; and thinking about worship is a different thing from worshipping." He goes on to say so disarmingly: "There is really some excuse for the man who said, 'I wish they'd remember that the charge to Peter was Feed my sheep; not Try experiments on my rats, or even, Teach my performing dogs new tricks.' "

This penchant for tidy togetherness and rational verbosity springs from the Scholastic tendency mentioned earlier to exclude the dark, subconscious part of the mind as a source of knowledge. This turns the Mass away from sacred mystery to sophisticated magic. It flirts with and flaunts modern man but does not exude or transmit the mystical life of the Church. If we keep people very busy at Mass and off all those silent and seductive avenues into the subterraneous caverns of the soul, we kill one of the most important possibilities the Mass ought to—and used to—provide: a rediscovery and revitalization of the Christian dream.

Worship, at its best, does not merely accommodate itself to modern man but sweeps him up into the self-oblivious, adoring act of the Whole Christ, from Melchisedech and Abel through Mary and Joseph to Bishop Austin Burke of Nova Scotia and Mother Teresa of Calcutta. It is the little human spirit's humble acknowledgment of the measureless glory of God, the only Reality—the Perfect, the Ultimate, the entirely Free. At worship we stand together, as did all our ancestors, dumbfounded and tongue-tied in the aweful presence of God, with the same deep unchangeable need to praise him. For this we need the universally pure and classic and majestic language of the Church. "What can I say, my God, my Holy Joy?" asks St. Augustine, "what can any man say when he speaks of Thee?" *That* is the spirit of worship, expressed socially and bodily because of our human condition.

*

Having grasped the significant relationship between religious experience and its theological and liturgical expression, we are in a position to understand what happens when the mind and the heart and nature and supernature are forced into an unhealthy and unhappy dichotomy.

We have reached a theological and liturgical impasse because we watered down the explosive and expansive dynamism of the true Christian ideal. Jesus' call to repentance—*metanoia*—was an urgent plea for a higher mode of consciousness, for a revolution in outlook, involving the whole man, heart and head. "Unless a man be born again he cannot enter into the Kingdom of heaven." There is no other way into the fullness of being human. Without the rebirth all other human advances lead to insoluble problems and bitter frustration; for instance, there's a person I cannot abide, a law I cannot keep, a virtue I cannot attain; perhaps I never will until I enjoy a higher mode of consciousness. St. Peter admonished the Jews: "Repent and be turned." The Nixon Administration fell into the Watergate mess, permitted governmental crimes, and refused to recognize the heinousness of it all because it lacked the genuine Christian viewpoint, a higher mode of consciousness than the political expediency to which it was committed.

Although rationalizations and abstractions still hold the day and the majority of us has only notional contact with the real, a strong reaction has set in, among the young especially. In fact, the other superrational part of the mind, for so many centuries repressed, is now in open rebellion. Unfed and unled by a wise, alert, prophetic, and contemplative Church, or by outstanding religious leaders, the rebellion against staid and stifling forms of religion has been thus far unproductive, and has remained unimportant, except as a symbol. Oriental faddism, Jesus Movement exhibitionism, and Pentecostal exuberance highlight a need but are in themselves no adequate response to the transcendental hunger of a starved people.

What these bizarre movements symbolize so significantly, however, is that experience is of capital importance. We live in an age of experiences. The transformation of the material world, the progressive control of life, revolutionary art, new efforts in all the realms of the spirit—violent, anarchic, perverted as well as proper—the upsurge of interest in mysticism: all of which indicates the degree to which we have plunged into a manifold world of experience. And so modern man inevitably asks: What worthwhile experience does Christianity offer?

Until recently the most pressing task in America has been simply to keep the faith alive, to hold the members within the pale of the Church, and defend them against abuse. Consequently, religious thinking has been predominantly apologetic. Catholics were necessarily exposed to a never-ending series of arguments about every detail of a complex creed, and children were prepared for life by slavishly committing to memory the questions and answers of the catechism and by an unattractive conformity. The tone of popular Catholic belief became almost entirely logical and intellectual.

We are no longer on the defensive. We must no longer live and speak in terms of reaction to Protestantism or communism, in terms of apology for our faith. This is no time to be immersed in threshold activities of the Church. We can no longer survive on such spoon-fed doses of religion. We must get into the heart of the Church—where God is experienced—or perish.

The Church is not a camp or a ghetto into which members gather and hide themselves and confine their activities for the purpose of peace, self-preservation, and incontamination. It is the framework in which Christ acts and reveals himself. It is through the instrumentality of all the organized elements of a diocese that Christ lives on among men, not for the purpose of coddling and consoling them, but to fulfill his earthly mission, which is to glorify his Father and save all men. The raison d'être of the Church is to gather all men into the life of Christ and commit them to his mission. To belong to the Church for any other purpose is to misconstrue its essence and purpose. The Church, at its best, is the whole Christ contemplating the Father and the Father's world. The Father's world, however, is not the package of illusions that lures people away from Christ's Kingdom. It is, rather, the redeemed stuff of life out of which the Kingdom of Heaven is made.

At the heart of this Kingdom lies an experience. It is time now to reflect on it in its specifically religious, mystical, and

Christian dimensions. The whole meaning of religious experience desperately needs clarification. We need to understand that religious experience is not something totally different from the natural aspects of the human adventure already described. Man is naturally religious. And his natural religiousness reaches a perfect peak and becomes a perfect exemplar in the "Everlasting Man," Jesus Christ. The Christian experience is the epitome of all human yearnings and, therefore, *religous experience par excellence.*

Chapter 6 – The Hunter and the Hunted

There is religious experience wherever there is living contact with God. It is a normal and necessary element in the life of religion. In fact, in its widest sense, it is synonymous with religion.

The religious experience of man before Christ was the experience of the *hunter* in search of God. The religious experience of man after Christ, in fact, the whole biblical experience, is the experience of the *hunted* man pursued by God. The relation of hunter to hunted is evident in the history of religiousness; it is important to recognize the value of each status and to acknowledge that everyman is both hunter and hunted.

Religious experience is expressed in various forms, crude or discreet, distorted or well balanced, disincarnate or integrated. Hence it can be found among "primitives" as well as among the "civilized." For too long now we have shied away from religious experience because we read or heard about neuropathic perversions or concomitants of religious experience. This, of course, was silly. Do we condemn sex because we know of morbidities, hysteria, and perversions that abound in the sexual sphere? It is equally ridiculous to reject religious experience as subjective illusion, when in power, satisfaction, and delight, and in its intellectual and spiritual value, it incalculably exceeds any other form of human experience.

An experience is thoroughly human and distinctively divine

when it means a total involvement of the person with all his human powers activated and unified, then suspended and transformed at their core by divine seizure. This experience is simple but implies very complex structures; it attains and puts in their proper order all the levels of human nature; it is composed of the network of relationships by which man grasps himself in contact with God. Such is the authentic Christian experience.*

Christian existence—that is, union with God through, with, and in Christ—is the primary element. As faith grows, the experiential element of our Christian existence asserts itself. It is due to a lively faith and appropriate psychological dispositions.

Our age-old tendency has been to cling tenaciously to the deposit of faith, acknowledge gratefully our union with God, do what we must to preserve that union; but do absolutely nothing to grow in the consciousness of that union, to identify with the mind of Christ and thus come to know God by experience.

The temptation of the man of today is to attach importance only to experience and to dismiss the faith. This is regrettable. Faith is not primarily a question of inner experience; faith is first of all a question of truth. What is required of me first of all, as a man of God, is not knowing what I feel, but knowing who exists. Only when I know by faith that God exists can I have a meaningful *experience* of God. Experiences, untouched by revealed truth, remain questionable and susceptible to multiple psychological, sociological, and other interpretations. Objective truth is the point of departure for everything. If Christ has not risen from the dead, any experiences that I may go through have not the slightest importance. The mystery of agape lived out in faith is the object of Christian experience. St. Paul emphasizes that it is an experience in Christ and in the Spirit that makes us realize our filiation and enter into the deep things of God.

There are criteria for judging this experience: It takes place in the community of believers, which is its necessary setting, its

* Except for his questionable notion of mysticism, this whole matter is treated masterfully by Jean Mouroux in his outstanding work *The Christian Experience*, New York: Sheed & Ward, Inc., 1954; also see Jacques-Albert Cuttat's superb study *The Encounter of Religions*, Desclee, 1960.

internal gauge, and to which it must always remain faithful. It implies the observance of the commandments, a humble verdict on self and charity toward others. Far from eliminating reasonableness, it demands it. St. Paul gives us a critique of charismatic inspiration, explaining the primacy of the spiritual; and the more he advances, the more he demands of the faithful a concrete intelligent grasp of the "mystery" of Christ. The major themes of St. John the Evangelist imply at least a vivid consciousness of the life, light, and love infused into the heart of the believer. And his first letter allows of no authentic experience except where the criteria are found together—ecclesiastical, dogmatic, moral, and mystical.

The laws we keep, the rituals we perform, the customs we adhere to, protect and enliven our religiousness. But the *soul* of religiousness is *prayer*. The whole purpose of the virtue of religion and structures of religion is to make us pray—easily and "without ceasing." Prayer, the penetration of reality, puts us in range of the Infinitely Real, in contact with the Ultimately Real, and in intimate touch with the Absolutely Loving Source of all that is. That is the literal meaning of religion (*religare*, to bind): to be at home again at "the infinite and inexhaustible ground of being" and therefore ready to be related and responsive to the Wholly Other who is always and everywhere making overtures of love.

God is pre-eminently apprehended where he dwells—in the depths of the soul. Although immanent, he is totally transcendent. Religious experience is not an emotion but an intuition, sometimes highly colored with emotion. It is not exclusively, not even primarily, subjective. It is not less but more rational than the mediate operations of the discursive reason.

"The Kingdom of God is within you." All great religious literature is a commentary on that; for instance, St. Augustine, prince of mystics: "I, Lord, went wandering like a strayed sheep, seeking thee with anxious reasoning, without, whilst thou wast within me. . . . Where was I myself when I was seeking thee? Thou was before me; but I had forsaken myself and could not find myself—how much less then thee." And the result of the discovery: "And I marveled to find that now I loved thee and not a phantasm instead." St. Bernard adds: "No one could seek thee unless he first found thee."

God is within us. He is more real than we are to ourselves. In some sense we are one with God. In fact, we are real only to the extent that we partake of the reality of God. "Mankind cannot bear very much reality." But we can know, see, touch, and clutch God, even though he is unknowable, invisible, untouchable, and inapprehensible. That is the paradox, and the alpha and omega, of religion.

We must dispense with all those things that get between us and God: that is the function of asceticism. The graceful but inevitable result is freedom to enjoy God: that is religious experience. What a silly and stultifying business it is to go through all the motions of religion and slavishly keep all the laws, but with no internal disposition of worshipful love! The objective holiness of doctrine and sacrament, which comes from the Living Holiness of God present in both, is only realized as an active force in human life when it is vitally apprehended and assimilated as living and personal religious experience. To act otherwise, subordinating the experiential element—that is, the soul of religion—to its institutional embodiment, its code and cult, is to let the letter kill the spirit. The work of the Church, the *opus Dei*, is not done until, through human interiorization of word and sacrament, the Spirit irrupts in a man, in many men, and the Incarnation of God, the Living Christ, is prolonged in the world. In other words, through prayer and discipline the ego will be reduced to zero. In the wake of the superficial, empirical ego, the real, substantial self will emerge and live in harmony with Pure Existence.

God is pure act; so that if he is present in the soul, he is also active there. We would know this if we were more intuitive, our lives more simplified, our personalities more integrated. The mystics are good examples of such powers of perception and presence. Mary, the mother of Jesus, is the best example of all. For most of us, unfortunately, supernatural life is a seed buried in the subconscious. But as we become less fragmented and dispersed, more single-minded and recollected, God comes closer to holding the central position in our lives, and the soul becomes conscious of that life within it. As God exerts more influence on the soul, the soul in turn becomes wisely passive—not inactive, but passively and positively engaged in receiving God, the Pure Act.

The human soul possesses of its very nature an obscure apprehension of God. It is so obscure that it cannot even distinguish its divine object. God is touched like an object in the dark, an unknown thing. If one grows gracefully in the life of the spirit, this contact becomes clear but confused; clear insofar as it is recognized as divine, but still obscure to the degree that it is still a presence and a plenitude on the edge of the subconscious attitudes and activities of the soul. The obscurity will always remain in this life, but with grace and growth, God's fiercely tender action, "the blind stirring of love" at the core of man's being, will rule and govern his whole existence.

In vital union with God, man sees his beauty and truth and shares his goodness. This equals holiness. The Divine Holiness is the ultimate religious category or quality apprehended in religious experience, God apprehended in his transcendent distinction from creatures—"thou alone art holy!" Man becomes whole by sharing God's holiness.

Religious experience must not be subordinated to secondary doctrinal insights, whose greatest value is their powerful reinforcement of the experienced union with God. But it must submit to reasonable interpretation, not for a pronouncement of validity, but for analysis and explanation.

The religious experience we live by is not merely our own, but the God-filled life of the People of God and the cumulative religious traditions of mankind. No artist, not even an artist of genius, confines his artistic knowledge to the product of his own aesthetic insight. Such a confinement on the part of a singularly endowed mystic would be just as absurd. He must accept the testimony of the saints, the teaching of the Church, and the universal experience of mankind. His own experience will not contradict the doctrine of the Church, which preserves and clarifies God's public revelation. But it will, hopefully, penetrate that doctrine so creatively and from such contemporary vantage points that God's "glad tidings" to mankind will be forever fresh and new as well as clear and certain. Such a prayerful and probing exploration into God is what Pope John called for when he introduced Vatican Council II.

It may be interesting to point out, as does Dom Aelred Graham in *The End of Religion,* that the three originators of three of the great religions—Jesus, the Buddha, and Mohammed—apart from the status later accorded to them by their followers, were the antitheses of official religious persons. Instead of upholding an existing tradition and declaring it sacrosanct, they criticized radically the established customs of their time and offered something more inward in their place. Each of us in his own life situation can make his own the words "You have heard that it was said to the men of old . . . but I say to you . . ." (Matt. 5:21–22).

*

There are peak religious experiences that result in a radical change of mind and heart, and will be regarded forever as definite landmarks in the deification of man. A good example of a peak instance of religious experience in the raw and its conceptual interpretation is Pascal's famous conversion experience, as recorded in the memorial he wore on his person until death:

FIRE
God of Abraham, God of Isaac, God of Jacob,
Not of philosophers or men of learning.
Certainty, joy, certainty, feeling, sight, joy,
God of Jesus Christ.
My God and your God.
Thy God shall be my God. Truth.
Oblivion of the world and all outside God.
Joy, Joy, tears of Joy.

Blaise Pascal, who lived in seventeenth-century France, a mathematician, physicist, psychologist, and engineer, was one of the great intellectuals of the world. His *Memorial* is a historical document in the strict sense of the word—a turning point and decision that stands in history, that engenders history: the inner Christian history of this man in that it brings to its culmination everything experienced up to this point and fixes a new beginning.

"Fire"—that is the raw experience with no commentary beyond the bare utterance. Pascal has stood in fire and experienced a real beginning, coming of course from a source other than physical nature or psychic consciousness. It was an experience of the spirit, the Holy Spirit: pentecostal fire.

Then came the staccato of words that highlight qualities typical of a direct religious experience: certitude, joy, and a new level of existence. But why does he stammer? Because he stands before the awful and the unbelievably new reality of God. It is not the God he knows about, the philosopher's God. His direct intuition of the absolutely, superpersonal being of God stands out in vivid contrast to the notional theism that is all that philosophers can attain without distinctively religious experience.

Pascal does not make this statement glibly, as we, who may know nothing of philosophical labor and the discipline of learning, are prone to do. Pascal was eminently qualified to make and understand the distinction. He had worked to attain the clarity and depth of true intellectual understanding, the precision and defensibility of a concept, the pure necessity of real insight into love and essences. One would have to grasp the enormity of the Christian insight of a philosopher and mathematician: that God is not the God "of philosophers and men of learning," but "the God of Abraham, God of Isaac, God of Jacob." What is being experienced by this towering man is the facticity, historicity, concreteness, and infinite freedom of God who cannot be had by man, but freely intervenes in the human domain whenever and however he chooses. The hunter is free to engage in the quest, but not in a position to find or to take hold of the divine prey.

"God of Jesus Christ." No other God. No projection. He whom

Jesus embodied. He whom Jesus meant when he said, "My Father." There is no Christian conception of God or Christian truth apart from the concrete historical Christ. What must be faced once for all is this: that the definitive category of Christianity is the particular, unique reality of the concrete personality of Jesus of Nazareth—who happens to be God.

In addition to this spectacular conversion experience of Pascal's there are other very influential but unspectacular kinds of religious experiences that occur frequently over a person's lifetime, even during one week. I can recall such experiences of my own happening in the Arizona desert, in the New York City subway, on the beach at Santa Monica and Malibu, in the lake at Nova Nada, at the Mellon Art Gallery in Washington, D.C., at a movie or a musical, reading a book or a letter, getting up in the morning (especially in Arizona), walking and eating with a friend, riding a motorcycle, watering the garden, baling hay, playing with the dog and the cat, watching Tessa comfort Siva in his long death agony, fetching water from the well, flying into Boston or Phoenix, driving down Route 1 in California, suffering physical pain, enjoying personal presence, watching my nephew being born and my mother dying, visiting the Blessed Sacrament, Father Ernie Ferland, and Mary Brodie, and most of all, celebrating Mass. Anyone who lives freely and deliberately cannot miss the deepest meaning and the sheer beauty of things and so come to know God by experience. But are not most of the experiences listed above of a sensuous nature? Indeed they are. Most religious experiences have a sensuous dimension. Most irreligious people suffer from an undeveloped life of the senses. Once the senses have been fully developed and have spent themselves in the service of the mind, then they are sometimes transcended in a more renowned type of spiritual experience.

In this feckless age of ours the senses need to be tuned and refined rather than mortified. How can you offer the world to God if you do not first take it in through the senses and make it your offering? Only a sensuous person can be "obedient to the voice of Being." In Martin Heidegger's striking phrase, "Man is not the lord of what is. Man is the shepherd of Being." How can we shepherd Being without a *sense of things?* We need to look at the world again with the eyes of a great delight, looking out gladly on the goodness of being. Matter *matters* before it *means*. "The senses," as Heraclitus said, are only "bad witnesses to those who have barbarian souls." "There is nothing profane here below," insisted Teilhard de Chardin, "for those who have eyes to see."

Life reveals itself in its images if we open ourselves to the image in such depth that we allow it to speak, as every image does, of its source. What is asked of us is not to disdain nor to dismiss images, but to purify them and make them open-ended. How else could a mystic such as St. John of the Cross be such a great poet? The Dark Night does not destroy images, it transfigures them. As Maurice Friedman, professor of religion at Temple University, points out, since God became flesh, he also became image. But in both cases there comes a time when "it is expedient that I go." And so although "the source appears dark emptiness," it actually

> brims with a quick force
> Farthest away
> And yet nearest at hand
> From oldest time unto this day,
> Changing its images with origin:
> What more need I know of the origin than this?
> —Lao-tzu, *Way of Life*

*

Religious experience does not belong exclusively to the Christian world. It corresponds to a basic human experience, common to all men, the natural knowledge of God. There are three dimensions of the human adventure: building the earth, communing with men, and the loving awareness of God. Skip any one of those levels of existence and you disqualify yourself from the human adventure. Try to achieve a civilization on a purely secular level and you construct a monster. That is why we find the religious dimension at the heart of human history. This dimension does not follow a consistent pattern of evolutionary *ascent;* on the contrary, due to man's freedom and frailty, there are periods and places marked by distortation and deterioration of the religious dimension. It is just such aberrations in our own Christian epoch that have made the Church so wary of any kind of "experiencing." Look at some of the disastrous instances in recent history: the Protestant crisis with its "experience" of justification; the quietist crisis with its "experience" of spiritual purity; the traditionalist crisis with its "heart vs. head" experience. But the divine spark in man is never snuffed out. In fact, the great scholar Professor Wilhelm Schmidt, in his gigantic twelve-volume work, *The Origin of the Idea of God,* holds that a primordial monotheistic conception of God can be proven in all cases as the underlying base, or rather starting point, of all subsequent religious developments.

In the broad sense, applicable to all men everywhere, religious experience is an experienced presence of a reality: a spiritual and ultimate intuition, invested with strong emotion, evoked by the *numinous.* Rudolf Otto, who analyzed these experiences better than anyone, lacked the exact word for this emotional intuition. But we have in English (for a change) just the right word: *awe*—a profoundly fearful attitude with no cringing. It is a *holy* fear—ontological rather than psychological, wonderful rather than gruesome. It is more like the fear of a benevolent ghost than the fear of a robber or a snake.

The response to the numinous is a mixture of delight and dread. There is sheer delight at having been *found by* God and in knowing that, despite our feeble and insecure hold on things, we belong to God; we are ultimately grounded, protected, and loved. But there is also terror because we have been *found out by* God. We are exposed to his holy scrutiny. We suffer radical amazement and embarrassment. And worst of all, our security is threatened because we are called by God from where we are to where he is; we are summoned into his unbearable presence.

This experience is, at least, the primary disposition for genuine religious experience. "The beginning of wisdom is fear." Man is led through his own experience of transcendence to turn toward

God. This is essentially bound up with his basic experiences of beauty, truth, love, and goodness. We discern someone alive in us who still transcends us. In an age as secular as ours the experience is often an aesthetic one. A kind of vague affirmation may be an initial form of religiousness, a natural response of man who is haunted by the divine, the supernatural, and is consciously or subconsciously in search of God. But it is far too amorphous to be an act of faith or a contemplative experience where the ravenous experience of the hunter becomes the ravishing experience of the hunted.

This vaguely pervasive and haunting presence of God is the dominant mode of religious experience common to the pagan religions and the history of mankind prior to the Judaic-Christian revelation. Man is naturally attracted by the divine presence who is the interior law according to which the world has its being. And this explains the glimpses of truth and of genuine knowledge of God scattered in the pagan religions among heaps of the grossest errors and moral degradation. The religions of India were characterized by supernal yearnings and pure glimpses of a Divine Reality, coupled with strange absurdities, gross magical practices, and false cosmological speculations. Even wilder vagaries dominated the religions of Egypt with their multiplicity of magical rites and texts (concerning life beyond the grave), their animal cult, their manifold gods, with henotheistic strains here and there.

Despite these persistent deviations and deformations, pagan religions did enjoy a cosmic revelation by discovering God in nature and in human gestures (birth, meals, family reunions, entrance into adolescence, the hunt, the harvest, engagement, marriage, death) and thus introduced man into the first stage of the spiritual life and prepared him for an authentic encounter with the living God. All people, including ourselves, must begin by being good pagans: recognizing everything as a veiled manifestation of God. The spiritual life of the Western world tends to be so dull, drab, and secularistic precisely because it is not pagan enough. The contribution of paganism, both in its ancient form and in the Orient of today, is positively significant. That is why recent *serious* encounters between East and West have been so fruitful. But superficial sallies into the East—by meetings, readings, pleasant sojourns—have often been disastrous, leading thoughtless and confused people into an overevaluation of the pagan religions, even equating them with Christian revelation.

Thomas Merton's contribution to the East-West dialogue is invaluable. Unlike most occidental interpreters of the Orient, Merton was able to de-Westernize his mind and disappropriate himself of all forms of spiritual imperialism and thus come to understand the Eastern mind, especially the Way of Zen. But even he, I believe, suffered/from an overactive mind and a certain religious restlessness. I sensed this in my conversations with him at Gethsemani, in some of his letters, and in much of his literary work. He sensed it himself, adverted to it occasionally, and at the end of his life, in the *Asian Journal*, referred to it with a certain painful, but still good-humored sense of regret: "I have a definite feeling," he wrote then, that the Asian trip "was something I didn't need to do," that there was "too much movement, too much 'looking for' something." Yet even to learn that, he felt, the journey had been worth it.

Superficial Christians, unacquainted with the deep, broad mystical life of the Church, or if knowledgeable, disinclined to take up the cross and follow Christ into the deepest and most rewarding mansions of God's mystery, are becoming increasingly fascinated by the religious peculiarities of the Orient, and are, consequently, flirting with an artificial and unproductive kind of syncretism. This is no more helpful than so many young people's mishmash conglomeration of all religions in a misguided effort to find a "religion with meaning." This whole trend needs to be stoutly resisted.

Resistance on this level, however, is not inconsistent with enthusiasm on other levels. The new understanding and appreciation of oriental wisdom in the West, our willingness to acknowledge the validity and greatness of Eastern spirituality, and our readiness—indeed, our dire need—to introduce into our own sloppy, uncontemplative lives some of their liberating techniques is a highly commendable mood of the day. Our weakness, for in-stance, is natural meditation and body-mind preparations for prayer, which very techniques are the strength of the East.

There may be no such thing as Christian Zen, but there are some "Zenish" Christians around, and a few of them are the most remarkable Christians of all. One of them is Father William Johnston, S.J., whose *Still Point* and *Christian Zen* are excel-lent reflections of Zen and Christian mysticism. With the help of Father Johnston I would like to show how helpful Zen can be to a Christian already steeped in and committed to his own tradi-tion. Father Johnston says in *Christian Zen:*

> Needless to say, we have Christ who I believe spoke of God as no man ever spoke; but I do not think we can claim to understand the revelation of Christ in all its full-ness. Perhaps we are still at the beginning. Moreover I also believe that in sundry times and in diverse ways God spoke to our fathers through the prophets, and these include prophets whose voices echo beautifully in the *Gita,* the *Lotus Sutra,* and *Tao Teh Ching.*

Zen teaches us first of all a methodology of prayer. The key to Zen is not sitting in a lotus position, but detachment. Craving is the chief impediment to spiritual freedom, as we have discussed in the "Human Experience" section of this book. Zen is ruthless as it presses on inexorably toward detachment from very deep and subtle things, such as the very process of thinking, from the images and ideas and conceptualizations that are so dear to Western man. The result is the unselfed Buddha nature—the object of Zenish faith, the unspecified goal of Buddhism, the patriarchs, and the sutras.

In Christian Zen the goal, clearly specified, is union with God: "I live, now not I; but Christ lives in me." The deepest and truest thing within me is not myself but God. In the end there is nothing except God. "There is no such thing as Jew and Greek, slave and freeman, male and female; for you are all one in Christ."

Christians can profit greatly from Zen methodology to deepen their Christian faith. And how desperately our faith needs deepening.

> The contemplative life is fantastically underdeveloped in the developed and affluent nations. Western civilization has become horribly one-sided and unbalanced, so much so, that serious people cannot see the distinction between a computer and a man. When this happens, and when the contemplative dimension existing in every man becomes starved, then people go berserk and do crazy things. And this is what is happening. Moreover, it is ghastly to think that it is happening even among some monks and nuns. Here are people whose lives are geared to *satori*, yet they feel that all is meaningless unless they are moving around the place making noise in the name of Christian charity.
>
> If young people look to Hinduism and Buddhism for the contemplative education that they instinctively long for, may this not be because modern Christianity has projected the image of a churchgoing religion rather than a mystical one? May it not have too much theological chatter and not enough subliminal silence? Words, words, words! Perhaps this is why we need the blood transfusion from the East. [*Christian Zen.*]

It is lamentable how extremely dualistic we've become: which trend is contrary to the long, central tradition in the Church of "a theology of negation," an apophatic mysticism, which is very close to the monism of Zen. The famous author of *The Cloud of Unkowing* says: "God is your being." And St. Catherine of Genoa: "God is more me than I am." This heavy stuff begins with Dionysius, the Father of Mysticism, and reaches a climax with John of the Cross, the Doctor of Mysticism. The seeds of this rich tradition are in the Bible, as we describe in the "Mystical Experience" section. Father Johnston fondly relates the story of Pompey who strode into the Holy of Holies curious to see what was there, and he found *Nothing*. This was the Jewish way of proclaiming the supreme unknowability of God. You find a similar apophatic vein in Job and Deutero-Isaias.

The practice of Zen might be a way out of excessive dualism and of coping more adequately with the problem of the One and the many. We should learn to behold the manifold in the One and lose ourselves in Christ.

> Dialogue in Christian prayer reaches its perfection when it is no longer "my dialogue with God," but "Christ's dialogue with the Father in me." That is to say, the real Christian prayer is not *my* prayer but Christ's prayer. It is the voice of Christ within my soul crying out, "Abba, Father!" How wonderful this is in Paul! In such prayer we have the nonself, since it is no longer I that lives, but Christ that lives in me. [*Christian Zen.*]

Zen is a state of Consciousness in which one sees into the essence of things. It is meditation without an object. Vertical meditation. Centering down. Superthinking. It enables one to be simply in the present, in the eternal now; and to look long and lovingly at the real. And all this may someday culminate in the transforming experience known as satori.

Superthinking helps to distinguish Zen or advanced prayer from the idling of quietism, a seventeenth-century aberration of prayer that suppressed thought and activity. Physical euphoria, whether it be quietism or a trip on drugs, makes no one wiser or better than before and does not glorify God. It is a wayward, fruitless kind of "Peeping Tom mysticism." Zen literature is strongly opposed to such things. In fact, Zen emphasizes work very much. To do one's work with total concentration and energy is one form of Zen practice. This reminds me of St. Teresa, who urged her sisters on and on: "Strive and strive and strive for you were meant for nothing else." The fact is that if you want to persevere to the end, you must rest in nothing. "Nothing, nothing, nothing," says St. John of the Cross, "and on the mountain nothing."

> This means renunciation, not of alcohol and tobacco, but of all thoughts and desires (even thoughts and ideas

of God), of all visions, sensible experiences, and the rest. *The Ascent of Mount Carmel* is a detailed catalogue of all things from which you must be detached, particularly those sweet spiritual experiences to which the mind cleaves. Unless a man renounces everything he possesses he cannot be my disciple. And everything means everything. How often people get attached to the joyful euphoria of their own *samadhi,* and they cling to it, they rest in it. And this, I believe, is a form of quietism that hinders progress. John of the Cross speaks of such attachments as the tiny thread around the foot of the bird, hindering it from soaring into the clear blue sky in serene freedom. A Buddhist author puts it another way. A man is standing in the subway leaning on his umbrella when the train lurches. He must let go of the umbrella and grasp the rail—otherwise he is lost. So let go of your umbrella. Let it go. Don't cling to it or you'll fall flat on your face. I write this to underline the radical nature of true mysticism, whether Buddhist or Christian. It rests in nothing; it is no search for a beautiful experience or thrilling kick. But let's remember, too, that renunciation is but one side of the picture. There is the treasure hidden in the field and the pearl of great price. To find these the suffering is worthwhile. [*Christian Zen.*]

John of the Cross and other mystics of the apophatic tradition are not intoxicated with darkness, as some critics, such as Frank Sheed, seem to think. They cherish darkness because it is the only sure way (tried and true) to the end (mystical union with God). All other ways are heavily mined with illusions, deceptions, empty slogans, and disguised idolatries. The darkness may last a long time (many years), and the end once reached may turn out to be infinitely deeper than anticipated ("eye has not seen, nor ear heard the things God has prepared for those who love Him"). And so the enlightenment of contemplation may not be characterized by titillation at all, but by a *deep stillness.*

As Father Johnston points out, one hears of stalwarts who have spent decades in assiduous sitting (*zazen*) without getting one shred of enlightenment, but this does not mean that they have been wasting their time foolishly. Dogen, founder of the Soto sect, insisted that the very sitting is a form of enlightenment, and this agrees with John of the Cross, who declares that the darkness of contemplation is in itself an enlightenment, even if one never arrives at any soul-stirring experience. Father Johnston finds this doctrine sound and thinks it is erroneous to dramatize the satori experience with lurid and beautiful descriptions. It is this error that has been partly responsible for a popular, ersatz form of Zen in America that is not very different from the kick one gets from drugs. The important thing in Zen, as in contemplation, is not the sudden shock to one's psychic life, but the total transformation of personality that ensues: the new *Christ*-man, the *whole* man.

From Zen we can learn some helpful things about breathing, rhythm, the koan, spiritual directors, as helps to Christian samadhi (the contemplative way). But the heart of it all is Christ. Even from Buddhism we can get new insights into our approach to Christ.

> We ought to be open to this kind of thing, because it is what our forebears did. Christianity, after all, began as a Jewish thing, but Augustine, Gregory, and the rest did not swallow the whole bit, hook, line, and sinker as it came from Judaism. These men lived in a Greek culture; they carried Greek insights into the Jewish revelation, and so Christianity grew and was enriched. Now if Augustine and Gregory did not take the whole thing from the Jews, I can't see why the Orientals should take it hook, line, and sinker from us. They will have their own insights, their own attitudes—and they will add a lot to Christianity, just as Greek culture added a lot.
>
> That is what I mean by saying that if we go to Christ through Zen we find him in a different way from the person who goes to him through Aristotle. I love that passage in Second Corinthians where Paul speaks of the glory of God in the face of Moses and the glory of

God in the face of Jesus. What radiant brightness and divine power is there! And do we little Westerners think we have seen all that glory? Do we claim to have exhausted all that wisdom? Far from it. In the face of Christ are myriads of contours yet to be explored; his voice speaks in rich and vibrant tones that Western ears have never heard; his eyes are pools of wisdom the Western gaze has never fathomed. And now it is the hour of the East to explore all this beauty and find what the West has missed. What an exciting adventure! But let me, a mere foreign barbarian who has spent twenty years in the mystic East, attempt to stammer some words about this new approach to the glory of God in the face of Jesus. [*Christian Zen.*]

Words, concepts, and images of Christ are not Christ. And so the author of *Christian Zen* pleads: "Let us reflect on the possibility that Christ can be known in the darkness, in the void, in the emptiness that transcends thought." He quotes an old *roshi* about words that are nothing more than a finger pointing to the moon.

And so the Zen dictum "If you see the Buddha, slay him" is not blasphemous nonsense but a way toward the purification of and detachment from images and a real participation in the Buddha nature. This is equally true of the Christian adventure: Get rid of images of Christ if you want the high contemplative union with Christ which is the real thing.

> Christ is the moon because the men who wrote the gospel are leading their reader to a vision not only of the historical Jesus (of whom we assuredly can have concepts) but of the risen Christ, the cosmic Christ, the Christ who was at the beginning. And it is he who escapes all images, all thoughts, all ideas, and all pictures. The risen Christ is so far beyond concepts that we find Paul struggling with all kinds of words to express the inexpressible. Here is Paul on Jesus.

His is the primacy over all created things
  For in him were created
  All things in heaven and on earth;
Everything visible and everything invisible
Thrones, dominations, sovereignties, powers,
All things were created through him and for him.
Before everything was created he existed
  And he holds all things in unity.

Don't let anyone tell me that Paul is here speaking about some simple reality that can be expressed in concepts and images! Nor is he speaking of Jesus just as he was in his earthly, pre-resurrection form. For Paul, Christ is a "secret" or a "mystery" or whatever you want to call it, and he keeps pointing one finger after another at the moon that no human eye can descry. The poor scholars get all tied up in Paul's fingers; the mystics turn toward the moon. [*Christian Zen.*]

We must not panic or clutch in the mystical heights. We must not lose our theological balance. We dare not cut the link between the cosmic Christ and historical Christ. The cosmic Christ is precisely the Jesus who shed his blood. And so we firmly establish as sturdy columns of prayer both Scripture and liturgy and an atmosphere of faith, without which the void might well become a literal void and not the rich fullness of mystical emptiness.

The man of prayer, the pilgrim of the Absolute, must begin with and be sustained sometimes by words and symbols; but he must press on toward the End. "And here there is no way, since for the just man there is no law" (John of the Cross). Then he will find, in St. Paul's masterly phrase, that his life is hidden with Christ in God. His self is hidden, Christ is hidden, and only God remains. But if this is you, remember that you will be there, very much alive; Christ is there very much alive; but you are not conscious of yourself or of Christ—because your life is hidden with Christ in God. Eventually enlightenment will come. Not any enlightenment, but the one toward which the finger points. Abba, Father!

*

Elements of Christianity are to be found in all mythologies. Christ is what they were feeling toward, fumbling toward, the answer to all their questions and fulfillment of all their needs; the answer to questions they had never thought to ask, the fulfillment of needs they had never arrived at feeling.

If we really understand the great religions of Greece, Africa, India, and Asia, we will see that the history of humanity is the history of successive revelations, each of which, despite inevitable regressions, constitutes a new advance in the knowledge of God through which a man is lifted up from glory to glory.

Prior to Christ and his "advent" time in the Old Testament, man who was a hunter, even religiously, was haunted by the sacred, solemn, unknown nature of the hunt. There was always something "spooky" about his religious style, in fact, his whole human behavior. This is still notably true of religious hunters (seekers) today who remain outside of the Christian pale, for instance, certain Eastern gurus who walk like zombies, pray like manikins, and talk *at* you in unctuous lucubrations. Spookiness even characterizes those religious sects that remain only on the periphery of Christian existence, barely influenced by the holy materialism and wise worldliness of the central incarnational principle of the Church, such as certain dreary amalgams of old-fashioned Protestant fundamentalism and modern, slick Catholicism.

The religious experience of the Christian is of a different and higher order from the most spiritual pagan experience. Christianity is not just another religion; it is not the religion of the West as Hinduism would be the religion of India, or Islam the religion of the Arab world. These ancient religions are the creations of man the hunter and the expression of the religious genius of a race. Christianity was directly revealed by God to man the hunted, hounded, wooed, and pursued. The step from religion to biblical and Christian revelation is a normal step upward and forward.

If the comparative study of religions is to have any kind of validity, it should discern not the true among the false, but the maturity of religion. Where is it full grown? One should be ecumenically irenic, but precise. So the answer is Hinduism or Christianity. Everything else was either preparation for, or vulgarization of, these two. Whatever you could find elsewhere you could find better in one of these. But Hinduism cannot be looked to as the most mature religion. For one thing, it seemed to be not so much a moral and philosophical maturation of paganism as a mere oil and water coexistence of philosophy side by side with paganism unpurged. The Brahmin went off to meditate in the forest while temple prostitution, sati, cruelties, and monstrosities of all kinds prevailed in the village a few miles away. Secondly, Hinduism did not pretend to any of the historical claims of Christianity.

Obviously, the Gospels are not myths. The mythical tone is gone; so is the taste. Myth is utterly foreign to these blunt, unimaginative Jews. But the content of the great myths is there, packed into their artless, historical accounts. If ever myth were to become a fact, this is it. This fantastic fact is unlike anything else in the history or literature of the world. And no person is like the Person it depicts; "as real, as recognizable, through all that depth of time, as Plato's Socrates or Boswell's Johnson, yet also numinous, lit by a light from beyond the world, a god. But if a god—then not a god, but God. Here and here only in all time the myth must have become fact; the Word, flesh; God, man. This is not 'a religion,' nor 'a philosophy.' It is the summing up and actuality of them all" (C. S. Lewis in *God in the Dock*).

Biblical faith is always connected with certain historical events. The faithful Jew, and subsequently the committed Christian, is not simply overawed by the numinous Elohim, the holy Yahweh; he is passionately and purposefully devoted to the God of our fathers, the God who called Abraham and brought Israel out of Egypt; and this historical emphasis is reaffirmed and developed in the Christian tradition. The object of faith is at once the "being of beings" of the philosophers, the Awful Mystery of Paganism, the Holy Law of the Patriarchs and Prophets, and Jesus of Nazareth who was crucified under Pontius Pilate and rose again on the third day.

Faced as we are with a worldwide religious upheaval and a theological eruption, it is imperative to rediscover and reiterate the heart of religion or the *backbone* of the Church. Some animals have a shell because they don't have a backbone. Once we discover and depend on the backbone of the Church, we will no longer have an essential need for its sociological and cultural shells. And we won't panic when every decade or so those shells are changed, scrapped, or devastated.

The spiritual reality that all men seek, intelligently or foolishly, consciously or unconsciously, can be found at the heart of the Church. The absolutely pure Spirit, the triune lovelife of the Godhead, is enfleshed there in Christ Jesus, the Risen Lord, alive at the heart of things: that's the backbone of the Church; that's where the (divine) action is. The Church is true to itself and helpful to others only to the extent that it ("she," actually, the Bride of Christ) remains at the heart of things. What happens there, at the still point, the creative center of the universe? Jesus prays to his Father in secret. That's what makes the world go round. It should also make us realize that we as individuals do not always have to come up with a red-hot prayer of our own. There is only one really effective prayer going on in the world. It's like the roar of a lion. It's the prayer of Christ marching through history with a single word on his lips—"Abba," Father—and a song in his broken heart, the eternal canticle of love. The Lord's prayer is going on full tilt. We don't simply imitate that prayer as if we were monkeys. We enter into it. We climb aboard the ongoing prayer of Christ, the great High Priest who in and through his Mystical Body and its sacramental life gathers up our tiny, scattered little efforts at prayer and gives them his own infinite value in the eyes of his Father and his own healing power over the wounds of the world.

If all I do is believe in the mystery of God and adore him in silence, I am a religious man, but no Christian. I become a Christian the moment I believe that God became a man, and that taking hold of that feeble human flesh, incapable by itself of bridging that immense abyss that separates it from divine transcendence, he transported it, in his own humanity, into the depths of God. And now I am in another domain, where God the Hunter has tracked down man and deified him; and now finds in him, his treasured prey, infinite pleasure.

What matters here is not an outstanding religious sense, but faith. How one feels at prayer is not a crucial question. "Is what the Gospels say true?" That is the important question. And one can surrender himself to that truth without any particular sentiment. Some of the most faithful people I know, live members of the Church, followers of Christ, defenders of the rights of God, are totally devoid of sentiment. On the other hand, I know people who effervesce so effusively (and disgustingly) with religious sentiment that they lampoon the whole spiritual life. Religious experience, though invested with emotion, is, I repeat, essentially an intuition. The Gospel truth is implanted in the intellect and the heart because Jesus Christ is recognized as a witness absolutely worthy of faith. The experience of things will follow from the word of the witness in whom we believe.

We have to believe in God, because of his reality, made lucidly and incandescently clear in his revelation, the decisive, fundamental Reality and life-giving Truth. This Truth cannot be proved by man (a divine truth can—but not this Truth); it cannot even be reached (searched for but not reached) by man. It reveals itself by taking hold of man. It is self-revealing; there is no other way to it. *The spontaneous self-revelation of the Living God who is Truth and Life is the only valid source of every authentic religious experience.*

Christ came to reclaim everything without destroying anything. All that previous pagan religious stuff was brought to a boil in Christ. Nothing was lost; all was fulfilled. Mount Carmel is a good example. This high mountain in Palestine was the dwelling place of Elias, the birthplace of the Carmelite Order and St. John of the Cross's symbol of perfection. But long before all this it was haunted by the priestesses of Astarte at the time of the Canaanite religions. Everything was transfigured by Christ. Easter recapitulates in itself the whole of religious history. It sums up the religious hunger and quests of the pagans and the Jews, and it brings it all to an end in Jesus Christ, in whom all things come together to ascend toward the Father.

There is something thrilling and imperious about the apostolic message. On the Areopagus Paul says, "Now God desires men to discard their ignorance and repent." His whole sermon there bears witness to the converging and subjugating revelation of God, given in Jesus Christ. The hidden mystery of God has been revealed unto us, "the understanding of the mystery of Christ which had not been announced to the previous generations of the sons of men, as it now has been revealed." To the Ephesians Paul continues: "And to me, the least among the saints, is given the grace to preach to the nations the unsearchable riches of Christ and to reveal to all, what is the dispensation of the mystery, which had been from eternity concealed in God, but now has been revealed" (Eph. 3:4–10). "Now the fulness of time has come and has to be realized and all things, in heaven and on earth, have to be united under One Head, that is Christ" (Eph. 1:8–10). Not long after, Paul Ignatius of Antioch wrote: "Ignorance has been abolished, the ancient Kingdom [of the Prince of the World] has been destroyed, when God revealed himself in the shape of man."

In view of the fact that Christ is the new and decisive revelation of the Divine Reality, it would be more accurate to refer to the experiences of God prior to Christ, or at least to the preparations for Christ in the Old Testament, as *quasi-religious experiences.* And it would seem equally correct to say that much of our current fascination with oriental religions is a form of religious regression.

In the Johannine Gospel, Christ is the Light: "the judgment consists in the fact, that light has come into the world, but man loved more the darkness." That is a basic sin: to behave as if Christ had not come, as if Jesus were not the Lord, as if he had not accomplished his mission, not as a Jew, but as Son of Man, as God-man. "It is consummated!"

"We have heard and seen and touched it with our hands . . .

and we bear witness thereof." Having "seen his Glory . . . Life Eternal," the apostles enjoyed a peak religious experience, an intimate fusion of transcendence and immanence. They were seized, not only from within but from without: by an inescapable and and objective fact. The salvation of the world lies in this fact, that Transcendent God became man, became near to us and like us, and that we are now "grafted" on him, the Existential Christ.

MYSTICAL EXPERIENCE

Chapter 7 – The Existential Christ

There is probably no more misused word in these our days than "mysticism." It has come to be applied to many things of many kinds: to theosophy and Christian science; to spiritualism and clairvoyance; to demonology and witchcraft; to occultism and magic; to weird psychical experiences, if only they have some religious colour; to revelations and visions; to other-worldliness, or even mere dreaminess and impracticability in the affairs of life; to poetry, and painting and music of which the motif is unobvious and vague. It has been identified with the attitude of the religious mind that cares not for dogma or doctrine, for church or sacraments; it has been identified also with a certain outlook on the world—a seeing God in nature, and recognising that the material creation in various ways symbolises spiritual realities: a beautiful and true conception and one that was dear to St. Francis of Assisi, but which is not mysticism according to its historical meaning. And, on the other side, the meaning of the term has been watered down: it has been said that the love of God is mysticism; or that mysticism is only the Christian life lived on a high level; or that it is Roman Catholic piety in extreme form. [Dom Cuthbert Butler, *Western Mysticism*, pp. 65–66.]

The word "mysticism" is being bandied about today in particularly reckless and outlandish fashion. It is used in reference to all kinds of meditations, to the performances of mediums and the ecstasies of saints, to sorcery, dreamy poetry, extraordinary psychological phenomena, esoteric human behavior, even, in the wake of William James, higher forms of intoxication, and since Aldous Huxley, drug-induced transcendence.

Such a ridiculously loose employment of the word merely confuses the inexperienced person who ends with the vague idea that every kind of supersensual theory and practice is somehow *mystical*. Hence the need to establish its true characteristics and re-emphasize the fact that mysticism in its pure form is the science of ultimates, the science of union with God, and nothing else, and that the mystic is the person who *attains* to the union, not the person who *talks* about it. The mark of the mystic is to be *held and captivated* by a personal, intimate, and experiential union with God, not just to *know about* it.

Mysticism, like revelation, is final and personal. It is not merely a beautiful and suggestive diagram but experience in its most intense form. That experience, in the words of Plotinus, is the soul's solitary adventure: "the flight of the alone to the Alone." According to St. John of the Cross, the mystic "enjoys a certain contact of the soul with the divinity; and it is God himself who is then felt and tasted." Mysticism is the only way out of human incompleteness and, therefore, the only way into the Kingdom of God, which is the fullness of being human.

There are two distinct sides to the full mystic experience: (1) the vision of God loved and (2) the moral transformation of the lover who with a wild and relentless passion desires to become identified and equated with the Beloved.

To become *conscious* of the mystical experience, one needs more than an apprehension of God or a passion for the Absolute. There must also be a fitting psychological makeup, with a nature capable of extraordinary concentration, an exalted moral emotion, and a sensitive organization of the artistic type. But this does not confine mystical experience to an elite. It was Eric Gill who reminded us that the artist is not a special kind of man; every man is a special kind of artist.

The mystical experience should be a *normal* occurrence of a *lively* faith. But the average man's life is so paltry and his faith so weak that mystical experience is in fact quite rare. This is deplorable. The first duty of the Church is to correct this dehumanized and desperate state of affairs.

The mystical experience is the deepest of all experiences of the deepest of all facts. Another word for it, in the fullest sense of this word, is *contemplation*. The fact—the most factual and concrete instance of being possible—is Christ. Contemplation is man's simple and total affirmation of that fact and the assimilation of this divine-human facticity into the depths of his being and into all the possible ramifications of his being-in-the-world. All other concepts of contemplation—pagan, pantheistic, platonic, hermetic, impersonal—were superseded and outmoded by the central fact of the human race, the Incarnation. Since then only Christian contemplation is a truly *mystical* experience. Just as all religious experiences were pseudoreligious prior to Christ, all very spiritual, supernal, even supernatural experiences were pre-mystical. This is not a narrow, jaundiced statement. It is more like the proclamation of a man who, upon discovering his wife in a yellow dress as bright as the sun, exclaims: "I have seen yellow for the first time!" Well, he who sees Christ, really sees God and man for the first time. This vision does not invalidate his former insights, whether of yellowness or of Godness, but brings them to perfect fruition. "Do not imagine that I have come to abolish the Law or the Prophets. I have come not to abolish but to complete them" (Matt. 5:17).

The result is not a bigoted parochialism, but *enlightened openness*. Recognizing Christ as the New Man, not another avatar or religious genius, establishes him as the One and Only Man with the Secret, hidden as the Bible says, from all other men and all other nations, and disclosed bodily in Jesus who recapitulated everything in himself and revealed what was buried from all eternity in the inscrutable and ineffable depths of the

Godhead. This is no limitation. Christ, the pontifex, bridge-builder, mediator, God-man, opens up the door to all the-ophanies; once you have Christ in fact, in the unmistakable and ineluctable lucidity and concreteness of his human existence, his humble, earthly countenance, then you will see him incognito in Asia, India, and Africa, as well as in the unlikely, unchristened places of the West.*

By designating the Christian life as the mystical life in the full sense of the phrase and distinguishing this tradition from all premystical traditions, I, by no means, limit authentic mysticism or the workings of Christ to the limits of organized Christianity. It is not difficult to recognize the same Christ who "before Abraham was, I am" (John 8:58) influencing (gracing) the scho-lastic philosopher Shankara's nondualistic interpretation of the Upanishads with the same spirit you catch in St. Paul and St. John, St. Catherine of Genoa, and St. John of the Cross. There are remarkable similarities of discipline between the Yoga Sutras of Pantajali and Teresian Spirituality or the Ignatian Medi-tations. There seems to be sufficient evidence of the hidden Christ of Hinduism to follow with confidence the lead of Dom Bede Griffiths, Catholic Benedictine monk living in a Christian Ashram in India, who seeks to find the presence of Christ *in* the Hindu Vedanta itself rather than in Christian dogma by way of the Vedanta. He believes, and I concur, that the insights of the other religions should make us Christians more capable of a comprehensive vision of the total Christ. This does not mean that Hinduism possesses what Christianity lacks, but rather that those resonances of the Word we do not advert to in the Christian milieu we may notice in a Hindu context.

So even though non-Christian religions, before Christ, were premystical preparations for what was to be revealed in Jesus of Nazareth, it now seems obvious that Christ, who has come and has already established his Kingdom in the world, is in some

---

* See Raymond Panikkar's *The Unknown Christ of Hinduism* (New York: Humanities Press, Inc., 1964) and Bede Griffiths' *Christ in India* (New York: Scribner's, 1966; published in England as *Christian Ashram*).

way sufficient to non-Christians, and is busy about his Father's business, manifesting himself to them, where they are, in their own religion.

We are harassed by the burden of living; exhausted, we look around for a place of repose, tranquillity, renewal. We would gladly rest in God and commit ourselves to him, so as to draw from him fresh strength to go on living. But we do not look for him there where he awaits us, where he is to be found, namely in his Son, who is his Word. Or else we do seek him because there are a thousand things that we want to ask him and imagine that, unless they are answered, we cannot go on living; we pester him with problems, demand answers, solutions, explanations, forgetting all the time that in his Word he has solved all questions and given us all the explanations we are capable of grasping in this life. We do not turn there where God speaks, there where his Word resounded in the world, a final utterance sufficient for all times, whose riches can never be exhausted. "God who, in sundry times and diverse manners, spoke in times past to the Fathers by the prophets, last of all in these days has spoken to us by his Son, whom he has appointed heir of all things by whom also he made the world" (Heb. 1:1–2).

The ineffable relationship of man to the Word of God is, to the endless joy and wonder of those who pray, always and simultaneously a turning inward to the inmost I and a turning outward of the I to the supreme Thou. God is not a Thou in this sense of being simply another I, a stranger standing over against me. He is in the I, but also above it; and because he is above it as the absolute I, he is in the human I as the deepest ground of it, "more inward to me than I to myself."

Yet the God who speaks to me is quite other than "my best self" or the archetypal world in the ground of my soul or some other thing lying deeply embedded in nature, its tendencies and potentialities. God is the Sovereign who elects and disposes according to his will; man possesses nothing to enable him with certainty to see how the determinate word will be uttered to him in particular at this particular moment in his life. From his nature alone man can never discern the will of God, the purpose of life.

This looking at God, the enfleshed Word, is contemplation. It is an inward gaze into the depths of the soul and, for that very reason, beyond the soul to God. The more the soul finds God, the more it forgets itself and yet finds itself in God. It is an unwavering gaze, where looking is always hearing—not something static but fresh and ever new—and so, as St. Augustine says, it is not enough to have received "insight" and "to know the testimonies of God," if we do not continually receive and become inebriated by the fountain of eternal light.

Mary owed everything to the contemplative fact that "she heard the Word of God and kept it," because she "kept all these words and pondered them in her heart." She is the model that should govern contemplation, if it is to keep clear of two dangers: one, that of seeing the Word only as something external, instead of the profoundest mystery within our being, that in which we live, move, and are; the other, that of regarding the Word as so interior to us that we confuse it with our own being, with a natural wisdom given us once and for all, and ours to use as we will. The idea of Mary as handmaid was too promptly superseded by "bride." Believing and hearing the Word of God are one and the same. Faith is the power to transcend one's own personal "truth," merely human and of this world.

All the concrete and objective acts and signs of God in history that man's faith must hold as true are simply acts and signs that tell of God's daring trust, presenting it to us as worthy of belief. God does not show us an abstract, theoretical, lifeless, dead trust, nor does he enclose the divine wisdom in so many propositions and precepts and leave it at that; he allows it to take flesh in the movement of history, of real life, with all its attendant risks. So he cannot be content with a dead faith as man's response. The Living God is present in the world and is personally involved for man's sake; he claims a response that engages the whole person, one given by man in his entire life as hearing the word and answering its demands. You don't gaze on the Absolute, but on the absolutely active, loving, engaged God.

God's gaze is primary. His looking at and knowing us is like the sun lighting up a landscape, giving it color, warmth, and fecundity, penetrating all things so deeply as to empower them to grow, flower, and bear fruit of themselves; but, all the time, they do so only by grace of the sun, which is the indispensable condition for such actions and the medium in which they exert them.

Natural mysticism and religion, which starts from man and is directed toward God, is an *eros* whose impulse is to take flight from and utterly transcend the things of the world, necessarily and inculpably. But in its desire to reach beyond the things that point the way to God, seeing them as messengers and intermediaries, it is in constant danger of losing the two, both the world and God as well—the world because it is not God, and God because he is not the world, who without the aid of the things of the world that mirror him, can only be experienced as absolute *void, nirvana.*

Christ rearranges things radically. The Greek concept of contemplation issued from the etymological definition: "Gather together into the Temple." In other words, come to the Temple with your contemplative minds full of pure essences and abstractions, with your mental powers so stretched and refined that you embrace intellectually the universality of being, and there in that sacred place offer all that magnificent freight of your intuitive life to the gods. Intuitive life, indeed, the worship of all those Greek heads full of abstracted truth and untarnished beauty, with no vital union with the good, the good old dirty world of definite people and tarnished things. Christ says: "I am the Temple." And the whole Gospel message has to do with living in him, being incorporated and transformed into him who is all in all in his own painfully human, earthy, sexual, historical existence. And so contemplation in the new, Christian sense is infinitely more than insight. It is a passionately willful union, an adherence, a fierce fidelity to the beloved. "If you love me, keep my commandments." The spiritual life or even prayerfulness is not a mental process but an individuating process whereby man, fetched and fascinated by Jesus, follows him into *mystery*: into the vision of his Father; and into *mission*: into the incarnational and ecclesial "leavenous" life of Church in the world. That is why St. Bonaventura defined faith as that "habit of the mind whereby we are drawn and captivated into the following of Christ."

But Christ returns from the manageable and imaginable world to the Father, and for the first time opens the way to pure religious contemplation. He does not abrogate the images and concepts that tell of the Father, which he himself also devised while living among men. On the contrary, he transposes them from the earthly, literal level to the heavenly, spiritual level, from the sphere of prophecy to that of fulfillment; and we who die rise again and are carried to heaven with him, are empowered by his movement from the world to the Father to accomplish with him the transformation of the old world into a new, spiritual, and divine one.

No mystic of the negative theology has ever traversed the "dark night of senses and the mind," which is the way to the absolutely loving and living God, so completely as did Christ. Neither has anyone experienced the passage from appearances to reality in more blessed fashion. Yet his death was no turning from the creature to gain God; it was God's rejection of all in the world that was not willed by God and did not conform to him. Nor was the Ascension a turning away from the world; it was an expedient departure with a promise of return before long, a departure to prepare a place with the Father to be occupied by men and the world as a whole, changed indeed and purified, but not repudiated or destroyed. And as a sign of his fidelity to the world, Christ, in leaving it, promised to send the Holy Spirit from heaven, who now that the Son's contemplation is finally perfected is to sow its fruits in the hearts of those who believe.

Jesus was so thrilled with Simon that he renamed him Peter. What thrilled him was his *Christian gnosis*: "Blessed are you because flesh and blood have not revealed this to you but my Father in heaven" (Matt. 16:17). The authentic Christian gnosis was almost eclipsed in the early days of the Church by gnosticism, a series of sects that laid claim to an esoteric and superior *gnosis*, or knowledge, than that of orthodox Judaism or Christianity. It is being smothered to death today by a similar demon, "psychidolatry," an inordinate fascination with the experimental conditions and possibilities of the psyche that preoccupies the person with such studied steps into self-fulfillment that the exploration into God is conveniently and respectably postponed.

The fascination with the demonic in modern literature, the tendency of many to turn psychoanalysis or "psychodrama" into a cult of self-realization, the illusory belief that personal fulfillment can come through release of one's deep inward energies and the more specific forms of modern gnosticism, such as at least one version of the analytic psychology of Carl Jung, which advocates taking part in evil as the road to the integration of the self—all these are popular diversions from the act of faith.

Psychidolatry, with its insidious relativization of values, pervades every aspect of our culture. It is not surprising that many men who have not managed to survive in the priesthood have moved into some branch of psychology. Psychidolatry, though, is not psychology or psychoanalysis. It is the subjectivist reduction that leads us to turn events that take place between ourselves and the world into psychic happenings within ourselves. Thus, love is not a crucial deep relatedness between two people: it is merely "good feeling." To psychidolatry, religion is either the projection of our wishes and illusions onto the cold and empty sky (Freud), or it is a purely psychic phenomenon—the integration of the self in the depths of the collective unconscious (Jung)—or it is a humanism in which God is merely a symbol of the potentialities of man, and religion a means to the end of realizing these potentialities (Erich Fromm).

One corollary of psychidolatry is the emphasis on *experience* and *self-realization*. Once a favorite and key concept of mine, and a perfectly good one, *experience* has got turned inside out. It used to mean looking at a beautiful scene; now it means taking a picture of it. We always want to possess an experience that gets in the way of addressing a real person or situation unselfconsciously or of responding with a single mind and purity of heart. People now talk about sex experience, drug experience, and religious experience in exactly the same terms. They are all comparable means of having an experience. Experience is now something inside of you, not something that seizes and transforms you. That is one reason why these same people can be so opportunistic, uncommitted, and unfaithful. What formerly was catastrophic is now casual—priests, monks, nuns, who were seriously and solemnly dedicated now leaving, marriage commitments and other contracts broken, friendships severed, new life aborted, simply because as these "liberated" people say, "I no longer feel comfortable with this" or "It's not where I'm at right now."

Another corollary of psychidolatry is the emphasis on extraordinary psychological experience. Mystical experience is entirely different from an extraordinary psychological experience. Experience phenomena are not even necessary concomitants of mystical experience. They are nothing other than repercussions of an experience that transcends us: more or less inharmonious reactions of human weakness under pressure of grace to which it is not yet fully adapted. According to St. John of the Cross, only the imperfect "have raptures, and transports and dislocation of bones. . . . For in the perfect, these raptures and bodily torments cease, and they enjoy freedom of spirit without a detriment to or transport of their senses."

*

The inclusion of the world in God cannot be effected except through Christ, who was the primary idea before the creation and on whose account the world as a whole and in all parts appears as it is and not otherwise. For "through him all things came to be, not one thing had its being but through him. All that came to be had life in him" (John 1:3–4).

Consequently every beginning of love that reaches out from the world toward God must let itself be transformed and integrated into the drama of this unique, distinct person, so as in him, to penetrate heaven itself, that is, to be delivered from the dim colorlessness of all that is merely of the world and take on a splendor of its own, worthy to stand alongside that of God himself.

This is the only way we can hear the Word of God: by being in the Word of God. We share the personal existence of the eternal Word of God. In Christ man achieves (is given) his Christian form and fulfills his mission. There is no other way to take hold of his destiny. The man obedient to his mission fulfills his own being. He could never find this archetype and ideal of himself by penetrating to the deepest center of his nature, his superego or subconscious, or by scrutinizing his own dispositions, aspirations, talents, and potentialities.

Christ is always to me the sign most actively opposed to the constant tendency of my speculative reason to deduce my religion from my own inner self. We find the convergence of opposites in Christ: the unifying of truths, of particulars, of the separate. He liberates; he does not constrict. He is the ultimate, and at the same time he is not. He is absolutely God and absolutely man, but he is also relative; for being the Son, he is a relation proceeding from the Father and returning to him.

Adam was the first mystic, a paragon of relatedness, in love with God and the world and in harmony with himself. He enjoyed this blissful state of mind until he got hooked on his own pride and avarice and started playing hide-and-seek with God. He then passed on to his children his own schizoid style of life.

We are those children, and we have forgotten that we are insane, as the following story illustrates:

> Once upon a time in a kingdom long ago and far away it happened that, after the grain crop had been harvested and stored, it was discovered to be poison. Anyone who ate of it went insane. The King and his advisors immediately took counsel as to what should be done. Clearly, from other sources, not nearly enough food was

available to sustain the populace; there was no choice but
to eat the grain. "Very well," the King decided, "let us
eat it; but at the same time we must feed a few people on
a different diet so that there will be among us some who
remember that we are insane."

The Bible is such a diet—a transcendent base, a center or
granary, *an order of reality that is "not of this world."* Men who
feed on this diet do not have to come out with bright, new programs every five years when they discover that in the meantime
man has come of a different age and the fashion has changed. The
Scriptures point them to that which is truly new and not merely
to a new arrangement of the old. Though the reality discovered
by biblical men is not *of* this world, it is certainly *in* it. This
reality is nothing other than God himself: and it is God *pro nobis*,
God active in the world, Immanuel, God with us. Living on a
biblical diet, therefore, is the only possible way to remain immune
from an insane form of acculturation.

Christian mysticism is the high point of the biblical account of
the love affair between God and man. The mystical dimension is
profound and pervasive in Sacred Scripture, beginning with the
human instrumentality through which God reveals himself in experiential ways. God manifests his presence at various times and
in many ways. Biblical history is really a history of mysticism. According to this history, the first mystic was the first man who is
described as Adam, not in terms of being an individual but in
terms of his uniqueness, his special quality as exemplar, his close-
ness and likeness to God, and his awareness of it.

Original sin, as described in Genesis, is a description of the
mystical downfall of man. To guarantee man's mystical life and
preclude the dehumanizing invasions of utilitarianism, which
would turn primitive man who was a man of leisure into a worker,
God told Adam and Eve to leave one tree alone. "Use the others,
enjoy their fruit, but leave this one alone." Why did God require
this of man—to mortify, restrict, or test him? No, on the contrary,
this was God's way of enriching man, of inducing him to exercise
all of his powers and live fully. Obviously (the history of human

ignorance and enslavement is evidence enough), the destruction or diminution of contemplative powers dehumanizes man. God's built-in corrective to the inevitable drift away from contemplation, the highest but most useless human act, was the *wasted tree*. Later on, one of the commandments given by God to another famous mystic on Mount Sinai would insist on one wasted day a week. Why? To take a long loving look at the tree with no useful justification at all, affirming and celebrating and delighting in the goodness and shining splendor of the tree with no concern for what we could get out of it. Such holy leisure and creative nonutilitarian action are the climate and the ground of the mystical life. And that is why Eden, the distinctively human place where one tree was left alone, was called the Garden of Paradise.

Adam and Eve, driven by some strange demonic force to dominate, to exploit, to use whatever could be used, to do whatever could be done, to become in fact like God autonomously, *used the tree* and lost their original privilege of being in the presence of God and in tune with the world. The rest of the Old Testament is a re-education and preparation of man for the restored human prerogative of the conscious pleasure of God's company through the gift of contemplation.

The gift was not completely unwrapped until Christmas, when Jesus was born and was able to say: "He who sees me, sees the Father." At that moment and ever after, the Greek concept of contemplation became inadequate, but whatever was valuable and true in the ancient notion was preserved and perfected in the *brand-new idea of Christian contemplation.*

High points of this education which lead to the "covenant" and then to the "law" and finally to Christian freedom can be seen in Abraham, who is guided and instructed by God, in Jacob's vision, in the revelation of God's name, in God's communication with Moses and Elijah. The theophanies of Yahweh granted to the prophets are always visions and also a vocation and a charge with regard to others. The preparation of mankind for the contemplative experience of God born of love reached a peak in the mystical lyricism of the Psalms and the exquisite Song of Solomon, the starting point of all bridal mysticism.

Throughout all the books of the Old Testament the spiritual interpretation issued from the self-disclosures of God: these were always historical, verbal, and universal—moving from the inspired individual to a wider circle, and finally to the whole people and to mankind through the covenant. Revelation was always eschatologically orientated to the end.

In the New Testament what formerly was shadowy and provisional becomes clearly and definitively real. All the adumbrations and preparations, the signs and myths of the Old Testament, culminate in the blazingly central fact of Christ Jesus as the mystic par excellence. His experience of God is unparalleled. It is the experience of God's own Son, God's own eternal and infinite experience of himself.

The Synoptics' account of Jesus and the early Christian experience of God in Christ is ingenuous, direct, and uncomplicated. And in Johannine perspective the existential and mystical dimension is unmistakably central and basic to the whole Christian adventure, for example, in the contents of the dialogue with Nicodemus and the Samaritan woman at the well. As a result of personal firsthand experience with *Him Who Is*, the fountain of living waters, "rivers of living water" flow from the believer and learner himself. The bridal theme also unfolds as God reveals himself mysteriously but intimately. No one is excluded from the offer that takes in the poor, the hungry, the afflicted, the heathen. And so it seems that the inspired writers of the Bible and all subsequent theologians have come closest to the truth when they referred to the God-man relationship (of *everyman* with the Other) in terms of bride and Bridegroom.

For St. Paul, too, Christian existence culminates in the experience of the mystery of God. His vocation is to announce to all the mystery hidden in God from all eternity. The attitude of mind we catch in the letters of St. Paul indicates indubitably a direct contact with God himself. Because the divine action is God himself in act, St. Paul discerns God is this action on his mind and will.

This is apostolic mysticism, meaning that Paul fulfills his mission as an apostle in virtue of a constant and conscious contact with God. The Divine Author of the "glad tidings" of the Gospels is at work in apostle and Christian alike, and if the faith of the recipient be sufficiently intense, he will be conscious of the divine action. St. Paul implies that the presence of the Christ-life within us is matched by an experiential awareness of the glory of Christ who is himself present in the life of the Christian soul.

St. Paul's whole life of prayer unfolds under the action of the Holy Spirit. When he cries, "Abba, Father," in union with the prayer of Christ, the Holy Spirit prays and groans within him, and he hears and is conscious of this prayer at the ground of his being. Paul's prayer is continuous and his awareness of the Spirit is continuous. His ecstasies, visions, and other charismata are only privileged moments when his contact with the Spirit becomes overpowering.

Mystical terminology, in the strict sense, first occurs in Christian literature in St. Paul, who uses the word "mysterion" as a key concept of the whole Christian message. And contrary to an illusion spread round the world, the Pauline concept of mystery had nothing in common with the pagan mysteries of Greece. The more recent studies of scholars such as Louis Bouyer, Lucien Cerfaux, and others have presented enough solid evidence to correct that mistake once and for all. The mystical experience is properly and peculiarly the Christian experience. Strictly speaking, apart from the mystery (of God in love with man) revealed and shared with us by Christ, there is no mystical experience. If St. Paul had spoken our language, he would certainly have upbraided his Corinthians for not being sufficiently mystical.

It is imperative—both scholarship and devotion require it—that we strenuously oppose the disproven notion that mysticism is nothing but a particularly noteworthy and also regrettable vestige in tradition of the Hellenization suffered by Christianity at the time of the Fathers of the Church.

The "love of God" spoken of in the New Testament is not the ontological nostalgia of Plato or the Greek hunger for the ultimate. It is God's creative, healing love; a love not of desire but of self-spending generosity; a love that gives its life, even to the extent of dying on the cross. This concept of agape as the fulfill-ment of eros is radically peculiar and original to the New Testa-ment.

Without ignoring other opinions I can unhesitatingly say with Father Louis Bouyer that the ideal of a "vision of God" in Christ, conforming us to his image, is purely evangelical and owes ab-solutely nothing of its basic elements to foreign influences, Greek or any other. The Gospels are full of mystical vision and mystical love. Let me just call attention to the striking formula of the pro-logue of St. John's Gospel: "No one has ever seen God; but God's only Son, he who is nearest to the Father's heart, he has made him known" (John 1:18). That terrific first paragraph of John's first epistle, proclaiming the apostle's intimate, experiential relationship with Jesus, has already been quoted. Two chapters later he reaches a diapason of mystical depths: "Here and now, dear friends, we are God's children; what we shall be has not yet been disclosed, but we know that when it is disclosed we shall be like him because we shall see him as he is" (John 3:2).

The Hellenization of John's Gospel and epistles is no longer held by the majority of exegetes. The Dead Sea Scrolls make such a contention impossible. The pre-eminently Jewish texts of the Qumran prove that all the biblical themes peculiar to John origi-nated in the Palestinian Judaism of the time of Christ. "What was pre-mystical in Neo-Platonism, not only went beyond the gross natural religions, wholly and carnally self-interested in their rela-tionship with God, but also certainly surpassed the mutilated Christianity which an anti-mystical Christianity would be," main-tains Bouyer. In her book *The Mystic Way*, Evelyn Underhill studies the mysticism of the New Testament. Writing to demon-strate that the Christian mystic has definite qualities that differ-entiate him from mystics who have evolved along other lines, oriental, Neoplatonic, and Islamic, she claims that this differen-tiation is acknowledged by such independent investigators as Leuba and Delacroix, and she sums up: "All the experiences characteristic of genuine Christian mysticism can be found in the New Testament; and I believe that its emergence as a definite type of spiritual life coincides with the emergence of Christianity itself in the Person of its Founder."

Mysticism properly so called is a purely Christian experience. Outside of the Church and Israel indications of it may be discerned that are remarkably convergent and yet are, if they have not been illuminated in some way by the Divine Word, lacking in the essential point. The point is to recognize the fact, still misunderstood though so obvious, that the very notion of mysticism is one that appeared only in Christianity, and that in it is distilled what is most essential in the Christian spiritual tradition. The history of the word "mysticism" serves to establish this fact.

Mysticism as a particular experience has been defined in reference to the "mystery," and not simply to any mystery whatever, but to the mystery of Christ and his cross, the mystery described by St. Paul as the great secret of the Word of God that the Church had finally proclaimed to the world. The use of the adjective "mystical" (in Greek *mystikos*, which simply means hidden) to designate a special religious experience is a purely Christian concept. This use itself is the product of a slow development that took place within the Church, a development that is extremely revealing.

Outside of Christianity *mystikos* pertained to the privileged rites of *initiates*. In Christianity it designated the most profound meaning of the Scriptures, a meaning accessible only to faith. For Clement or Origen, the mystical sense is the full sense in which all the lines of revelation converge. This is what St. Paul calls the "mystery": "Jesus Christ and him crucified," but more particularly, the cross of Christ seen in all its effects; what Paul again calls: "Christ in us, the hope of glory."

The first act of charity springing from faith, a faith nourished by the sacraments, contains in embryo the whole of mysticism. The mystical development of every Christian life carried to holiness will be more or less conscious according to the innate tendency and capacities of the subject for reflex consciousness of what is going on within him. You can have mystical life without talk or being aware of it. For there is no sanctity other than this "unity of the Spirit" with the Holy Spirit living in us, which is described by William of St. Thierry as the height of the Christian life, and which is a good description of mysticism made perfect.

Chapter 8 – The Earthy Mystic

The contemplative life increases in proportion to the activity of God within us, our own perception of which constitutes the supreme experience of the Christian life. This experience of God within us has been called in traditional Christian language *mystical*. It is not an experience that can be reproduced more or less at will ("Let's have a bash at Esalen, Pecos, the Arica Institute"); neither is it something that can be observed as if from without by the experimenter himself. It is neither achieved nor controlled. It is not the product of any method mastered by appropriate techniques. There is no way to test and measure the experience while wholly given to it. This touch of God is bestowed gratuitously in the worshipful act as self-oblivious engagement.

What constitutes mystical knowledge as the highest expression of religious experience is that it is a form of knowing without any intermediary: here we know God through his own presence and his own activity in us.

There is a most unfortunate tendency today to reduce God to love of neighbor. There is no way for me to prove the point here; but it would not be difficult for a historian to show how this proclivity toward an exclusive preoccupation with "interesting and exciting inter-human-relationships," a purely horizontal spirituality, characterizes all the notoriously weak ages of the Church. The strong ages are consistently mystical. Our own epoch is obviously an effete period. Hopefully we will become strong. There are reasons for hope.

But the horizontal tendency prevails, and it is in opposition to the Gospels, to tradition, and to the enlightened teaching of the mystics. Love of neighbor is certainly the *touchstone* of the love of God, but it is not *equivalent.* St. John in his first epistle emphasizes both but does not reduce one to the other: "We love because he loved us first. But if a man says 'I love God,' while hating his brother, he is a liar. If he does not love the brother whom he has seen, it cannot be that he loves God whom he has not seen. And indeed this command comes to us from Christ himself: that he who loves God must also love his neighbor" (I John 4:19–21). The whole Bible is so lightning clear and thunderously emphatic about the first two commandments and the primacy and specificity of the first; especially the Gospels where the love of neighbor is presented as the consequence of a primary and fundamental love *for God himself* (cf. Matt. 12:37, Mark 12:30, Luke 10:2). In fact, as Louis Bouyer points out:

> If we admit that our participation in the love, the *Agape,* of God is reduced to an active love of neighbor, not only do we return to a natural plane and even a pagan one (as the opponents of Christian mysticism very lightly accuse it of doing), but, as must be admitted, we descend far lower in the natural religion of fallen men than the level attained by Greek contemplation, at least in Neo-Platonism. In fact, whether we realize it or not, a religion —however purely evangelical it wishes to be, however suspicious it may be as to any foreign infiltration that might adulterate it—which concerns itself with God only for the good of man actually goes back to magic. For if our religion, our life of prayer, has no other aim than the transformation of the world, the betterment of human life by drawing divine benefits down upon it (by what is called "prophetic prayer" in unwarranted contrast to "mystical prayer"), then whether we wish it or not, whether we know it or not, our religion rejoins that of the Canaanite Baalim against which the prophets never ceased to inveigh. For then, whatever our pious verbal

protestations may be, in practice we reduce God once more to a mere source of energy to be exploited in interests of man. [*Introduction to Spirituality*, p. 226.]

This preoccupation with God as he is in himself is the mystical life.

What then is the difference between a religious experience and a mystical experience? An example occurs to me. One day some friends came to my house looking for me. I hid in the closet. They happened to hear the noise I made climbing inside. Although they didn't see me, they knew I was there (figuring it had to be me!). We were all present in the same little house together. And so with joyful excitement and heightened anticipation mingled with fearful trepidation, they began to seek out my exact whereabouts. To them, the most real thing, certainly the most influential at the moment, was my unseen presence. Well, *that is what a religious experience is like.* Finally they opened the closet door, saw me standing there, and even though they knew what they were going to find, when they saw me with their own eyes, came into direct contact with my actual bodily presence which was until that moment merely a suggested presence, a haunting, telltale noise in the room, they stood still and screamed. *That is what mystical experience is like.*

It is time to summarize the whole gamut of experience from beginning to end. The *human experience* of contemplation (seeing the Real) and vital union (enjoying the Good) becomes *religious experience* when God is recognized as the ultimate subject of the contemplative union. Religious experience becomes *mystical experience* when the direct object of perception is no longer the self, the other, or the event, but the "mysterium" that suffuses them and underlies the phenomenon. The mystical experience becomes *Christian* when Christ is seen to be the Way into the mystery, in fact the mystery itself, since he is not only the way but the truth and the life as well. The *psychological constituent* of the mystic consists simply in this: that he is obviously a mystic. All saints are mystical, though not to the same degree. The fact that some are easily recognizable mystics is due to their peculiar type of temperament.

For centuries man was haunted by the presence of God in the world. But not until Christ—"that which we have seen with our eyes and which we have gazed upon and our hands have handled" —did man have in the full sense of the word a mystical experience. The *mystery* of the Godhead is revealed. The mysterious Presence sensed by religious men for all those centuries is now connected with a definite historical Person, manifested in the flesh, Something, or rather Somebody extremely concrete, definite, and unique—and this was the Word of Life, the Life Eternal.

That is why there is nothing *spooky* about the Christian saint. He is an *earthy mystic*. That is the necessary and characteristic mark of the incarnational spirituality of the West: earthiness, or ordinariness, or even worldliness. Who are the greatest mystics in the history of Christianity? Mary and Joseph, who became saints by taking good care of Jesus. They had no mystical techniques. Their lives were unpretentious, almost unnoticeable. Every one of the apostles was a mystic; they were rugged, untutored fishermen, not theologians or philosophers. But they stayed close to Christ, were caught by his good infection, saturated with his Spirit—the *mystery* of Triune Love.

Their whole training and their subsequent apostolate began with a mystical experience. John, the beloved disciple, has witnessed to it. What he once touched and tasted and handled, *that* he has declared to us. It was the shining and the glowing of God's own beauty in their midst, in the body of Christ. "We saw his glory, the glory of God himself." It all began the day that quiet but majestic figure of Jesus passed by, and the Baptist yelled out: "Behold the Lamb of God." Two of the fishermen and John the Beloved, who tells the story, dropped what they were doing and followed him. They knew that this was a man "who spoke like no one ever spoke," *a man with a secret*. They were determined to wrest that secret from him. So they took off after him. The stranger knew they followed and turned to them and looked upon them with a look that could pierce a man's inner depths and transfigure him. It was when he turned to them that they heard his voice first speak—that voice which by its cry could raise the dead. "Whom do you seek?" That was all. The fishermen hardly knew what to say—only they must see him, must go with him, and so they stammered out, "Rabbi, where do you dwell?" And he said, "Come and see." A very quiet but gripping encounter. Nothing dramatic; no big dialogue; just a few words of salutation; three short sentences that could be said in half a minute. And yet they sealed their lot for eternity. That was an invitation to contemplation. "Come and see." They went and saw, and learned firsthand who he was, and though they could not force the secret from him, he began to share with them the "glad tidings." So intense is the apostle's memory of that high time that he can never forget the very hour of the day. It was just ten o'clock when they got to the house. They stayed with him long enough to know him by experience. Then he sent them away with his words burning on their lips and his love blazing in their hearts.

That's the literal meaning of *apostle:* "to be sent." That apostolic tradition has endured. The only authentic apostles in the world are those who have been sent. The rest are phonies. And the only people God sends are people whom he has already reached, touched, and begun to transfigure. Apostles are not perfect. They are—we all are—sinners; but they are *touched* sinners. They are divinized by his touch; "virtue went out from him." J. D. Salinger summed it all up neatly when he said: "See Christ and you are a Christian, all else is talk." Real apostles represent Christ more by radiance and dynamism than by words. What they represent is much more readily caught than taught. It is contagious.

The effectiveness of a man's apostolic work depends upon the reality and intensity of his mystical life. No one can give what he does not have. One silent, solitary, God-centered, God-intoxicated man can do more to keep God's love alive and his presence felt in the world than a thousand halfhearted, talkative, busy men, living frightened, fragmented "lives of quiet desperation."

It has been popular for some time now to designate Christ, essentially, as *the man for others*. This is a fallacy. Christ was indeed the most altruistic man who ever lived. He spent himself and emptied himself for the others. "And greater love than this no man has, than to lay down his life for a friend." Yet essentially he was not the man for the others; he was *the man from the Wholly Other*. It was this ruling attention to and absorption in his Father that defined and identified him and empowered him to be crucified for the others. So Jesus spent most of his life unknown, in solitary communion with his Father, the holy, ineffable, mysterious, One. Even during his brief active period, his worldly career, he could not resist the pull and dynamism of his Father, the tug of his roots that lay in other worlds; and so he was forever returning to the desert and the mountaintop. He seemed to linger too long in sacred places such as the Temple and would have to defend himself: "Did you not know that I must be about my Father's business?"

Christ emphasized contemplative action rather than theological speculation. In multifarious ways Jesus reiterated his central theme: You cannot know God unless you belong to God. And without spiritual formation and contemplation there is no belonging.

We learn something important about the use of verbal instruments from the Word made flesh. What a laconic Word he is. Words are supposed to speak, but he says little, and then says almost nothing new. It turns out that the Word does not philosophize or theologize much at all. He makes acts of love, comforts, heals, inspires. His sparse words are personal, vocational, challenging: come, follow, see, love, taste, suffer, die, be reborn. He seems repelled by definitions. He answers questions not by correct formulations but by courageous action. He seldom uses nouns: they are too neat, tidy, categorical. When he does use a noun, it is usually a singular instead of a plural. He does not talk about beliefs; he calls for faith. He does not preach virtues; he evokes love.

What he *does* is his word. He is what he does. The infinite and ineffable God makes himself known not by preachments, but by presence through action. The thing Christ stated was active and lively enough to be called a dance. And wherever and whenever there is a new exchange of love, the Christian dance continues.

People kept trying to draw Christ into a tangle of words, to explain things, to solve intellectual problems; but he resisted and drew them instead into a web of his love. "Taste and see" was his answer to all their questions. Once his followers got a taste of his personal Truth, they became progressively fascinated and ultimately consumed. After all, as François Mauriac said, once you get to know God you cannot be cured of him. And St. Teresa assures us that all of our trouble comes from not keeping our eyes on Christ. The apostles became mystics by becoming Christ-men.

We become mystics the same way. If you want to get warm, you get in the sun; if you want to get wet, you get into the water. If you want divine life, the mystery of love, you get into the one living organism in this world that has it—the Mystical Body of Christ. That's where mystics, the people who know God by experience, are born: in the womb of the Church; not on the periphery or on the edges, certainly not in the outskirts, but at the center of the Church where the infinitely attractive personality of Christ is revealed and the meaning of everything else becomes clear; and man, in touch with the All, becomes so ontologically humble and in harmony with the universe that he becomes willing to let God be God, and only God be God.

Whoever is alive to God at the heart of the Church is a contemplative. Whether you are in the city or the desert, a monk or a milkman, a nun or a nurse, does not matter. What does matter is that you are living *deeply* enough to be quickened by the mystical life; the mystical life that is generated from all eternity by the lovelife of the Trinity, that sprang up in our midst when Jesus walked on the earth, and that now flows like deep water at the deep center of the Church.

It is at this deep center of ourselves and of the Church that God says, in the words of the Psalmist: "Be still and see that I am God." At the center—that's where the action is; and it is the highest and the most fruitful kind of action. We are always trying to change reality, manipulate it, master it. We should use all that energy to change ourselves in order to see reality. As Baron von Hügel once said, we need "inward and shrouded men" in whom the Word of God does not turn into action but to "simmering deep-down fermentation."

Although it is not the common opinion, the mystics of the West are, in fact, the most practical of all men. Aldous Huxley is absolutely right when he says in *Grey Eminence:*

> The mystics are channels through which a little knowledge of reality filters down into our human universe of ignorance and illusion. A totally unmystical world would be a world totally blind and insane. From the beginnings of the eighteenth century onwards, the sources of all mystical knowledge have been steadily diminishing in number, all over the planet. We are dangerously far advanced into darkness.

People are fed and sustained by a mystical theology. They are amused and confused by any other. People are being led thoughtlessly from one vogue to another. Now, for instance, it's the "inner city." That's where the action is, and God is where the action is. But Christ said: "Where two or three are gathered together in my name, there I am in the midst of them"—suburb, mountaintop, beach, attic, bar—it doesn't matter.

It's tempting for the theologian to be faddish, accommodating; to leave his solitary, silent stance before the source of Wisdom and become washed out in the "sauce" of endless meetings, parties, dialogues, lectures, conventions. It's so easy to blame the old myths, symbols, structures. But where does the trouble really lie? In our routine, barren experience of Christian truth. If we would really immerse ourselves in the Christian existence and discover ultimate reality—God—with the whole mind, then this Truth would become our own inner truth and be transmuted into terms and symbols that would reach our contemporary fellowman. Such a mystical theology would make the pseudoscientific religious jargon, valid for the next five years, look silly. What is required of Christians is that they develop a completely modern and contemporary consciousness in which their experience as men of our century is integrated with their experience as children of God redeemed by Christ.

People would serve theologians best by pleading with them in the words of François Mauriac:

> I would like to be assured that they are not too much affected by what is "of the day," they from whom we ask the words of eternity. . . . I confess that it does not interest me in the least to know what my friends in Orders think about the Marshall Plan, the Revolution in Technics, or the Crisis of the French Cinema. . . . the purpose of these religious in the world of today is to maintain a guidepost, is to say over and over again untiringly in the name of their Master: "I am there, I am always there." . . . How ill adapted they are to the world whose language they do their utmost to speak. How one would like to cry out to them—but most certainly not as an affront—on the contrary, as praise: "Attend to what concerns you, to Him who concerns you, Him whom you concern; initiate yourself into the secret of contemplation. . . . How avidly I would listen to them, if they spoke to me of the Son of Man, not as theologians, not as sociologists, but as those who see, who touch the Resurrected Christ. [*The Stumbling Block.*]

We must learn to be *earthy* mystics, progressively fascinated by the incognito Christ. Wherever we are, whatever we are doing, we must learn to be still, to look and listen and absorb and enter into the mystery of things, the mystery of an airplane, a mountain, a lake, a poem, a blade of grass, a symphony, a cat. Our nation is more threatened from within than from without. The mind needs to feed on mystery, on the poetry of life, as the body needs to feed on food. That is why in education, as in life as a whole, the things of greatest value, of greatest importance, are the useless things, the time-wasting things that don't enrich our lives materially but do make man worth saving and life worth living.

On a famous occasion Mary of Bethany was commended by our Lord for doing nothing. Martha was very busy getting dinner. Mary was sitting still, looking, listening, learning—learning God by experience, by association, by love, which is the most direct and immediate kind of knowledge of God. In our utilitarian judgment Mary was doing nothing. But in our hearts we know which of the two sisters was in fact wasting time, wasting her opportunities. Being alive to God and his world! That's the most important thing in life, and that's what Mary was doing.

Right from the opening of Genesis to the end of the Bible, one thing is clear: that true vitality is God-given; wise activity, fruitful activity is Spirit-inspired. We have lost the biblical perspective in our pretentious, hyperactive, man-centered, spiritual(?) programs. And yet our Lord tells us unequivocally that to have true life within us, we must be born anew, from on high, born of water and the Spirit.

We submit to the water all right but not to the energizing quickening, transforming Spirit. And so, despite our clever thinking, our relentless pace, and our ceaseless activity, we cannot lift ourselves out of our chaos and absurdity. St. Paul says the same thing: "They alone are the children of God." There is no other way—however busy and efficient and religious we may be—to the full life.

The truly human person, the wise man, the earthy mystic, does not only learn about God and divine things, he "enjoys" or "suffers" God by experience, by personal encounter. We are not really practical, and we shall get nowhere, we shall never find life, life will escape us, unless we learn not to be always bustling about—unless we learn to be still, to let things happen around us, to wait, listen, receive, contemplate.

Only after we receive God's Word can we be articulate; otherwise we stammer and stutter and beat the air. We entertain or bore people to death, but we cannot communicate the Word. Unless, having disposed ourselves through prayer and contemplation, we receive life from the creative power of God, we cannot engage in fruitful human activity.

That is why activity without contemplation is blind. Louis Lallement, reliable spiritual guide, says: "If we have gone far in prayer, we shall give much to action; if we are but middlingly advanced in the inward life, we shall give ourselves only moderately to outward life; if we have only a very little inwardness, we shall give nothing at all to what is external. A man of prayer will accomplish more in one year than another in all his life." A generation before Lallement, St. John of the Cross, the greatest and most reliable of all spiritual guides, the mystical doctor of the Church, said that those who rush into good works without having acquired through contemplation the power to act will accomplish little more than nothing, and sometimes nothing at all, and sometimes even harm.

St. Ignatius insisted that even in the apostolic labor of public ministry, the "Apostolate of Prayer" be placed above all external activity. "For the attainment of the end . . . the help of souls . . . such means as unite the instrument to God are more effective than those which dispose the instrument towards men. . . . The former are the interior means which must impart efficacy to the external means we employ in attaining the end proposed to us."

These strong statements are not against activity. In fact, they are compatible with very intense activity and favor such attitudes as that expressed superbly by Cardinal Giacomo Lercaro: "God forgive me if I am not exhausted at the end of the day." What the spiritual masters are against is *feverish* activity—a self-directed, unprayerful, fretful, noisy, pretentious kind of activity full of human energy without divine impetus and charity. And—I cannot say this emphatically enough—it takes more than intention to be actively engaged under the dominance of the Holy Spirit. It takes a sturdy (note, I did not say rigid) discipline of life, a contemplative life; not monastic, not enclosed, not aloof from the world, not inactive, but contemplative. I am sure we are going to have to repeat this countless times and explain it again and again because the principle seems new to our Western society, though actually it is as old as the world. "And the Spirit brooded over the waters. . . ."

Some who favor the activism we are used to point to the active saints as proof of its validity. But in every single case it was con-templation that drove these saints into action, just as it was con-templation received in prayer and solitude that sustained, mo-tivated, and crowned their activity. The more active they became, the more prayer they added. This was not too difficult because they had already acquired the habit of prayer. But the acquisition of the habit of prayer takes time, regularity, discipline, direction, silence, and solitude.

It is true that saints such as the Curé of Ars, John Bosco, Joan of Arc, and Thomas More sought God in their neighbors from morning till night, but they spent even more time from morning till night, and sometimes through the night, seeking God in him-self—absolute, absorbing, transcendent. After all, if God is real, then he must be the captivating, compelling object of our rapt loving attention for the rather long, solitary periods of our lives. It is not enough to talk about him (even this is often a subtle escape from him). We must face him, address ourselves to him. This confrontation with the real, live, personal God is the most real part of a man's life. Never is he more a man than when he prays. It is a highly significant fact that the perfect man with in-finite talent, Christ, spent most of his life in prayer. This fact ought to influence our apostolate much more than it does. St. John of the Cross, a very active man himself, said that one act of pure love of God is worth more than all other activities (preach-ing, teaching, etc.) put together.

The people who hunger most for contemplation today are the men and women who are most actively engaged in the apostolate. And no man can live a deep spiritual life without long, lonely periods of thoughtfulness and love in the presence of the Lord. Our most active apostles today have discovered that no man can communicate effectively with other men unless he has already learned to hold personal, solitary communion with God. And so today just as yesterday and always man's most ardent plea is the same: "Teach us to pray."

Christ not only teaches us to pray by the words of the Our Fa-ther but also by the sacrament of his own prayer life perpetuated in the world by his body of believers, the Church. The prayer life of the Church is the prayer of Christ in the contemporary world, and is, consequently, the only valid source and true pattern of all personal prayer.

The mystical life of the Church, then, is her *re-enactment* of the mystery of God's love, agape, embodied in the life, death, and resurrection of Christ. The liturgical life of the Church is her public, symbolic expression of that deeply *interior* re-enactment of Christ's sacrificial life and glorious resurrection that is unfolding creatively and redemptively in the rather ordinary daily lives of Christians everywhere.

We are all caught up in the exhilarating *passover* from slavery to freedom. The liturgy is our celebration of the outstanding liberating landmarks on our route to freedom. At Baptism we rebel against and sever our relationship with the enemies of God and accept the Godward dimension. At Confirmation we pledge our allegiance to God and commit ourselves to the services of love by the power of the Holy Spirit. In the Eucharist we celebrate our union with God. Notice how the rhythmic patterns of growth in the liturgical and mystical life are the same. That is because the single life of the whole Church, the people of God, is both liturgical and mystical simultaneously. And so we move from baptismal purgation through the illumination of the Holy Spirit at Confirmation into the unitive way of the Eucharist.

We follow the same mystic route in every single Mass we offer. We begin with purgation at the foot of the altar. We stand there humbled and penitent, as sinners, slaves, lawbreakers, unprofitable servants. We need a Savior God, we need forgiveness; we need to be liberated and detached from all our inordinate attachments. Our first step toward the summit of holiness and freedom, the pinnacle of perfect love, is to keep the commandments, to become honest-to-goodness, down-to-earth, reliable, faithful servants of God. "If you love me, keep my commandments." Keeping the commandments is not the big thing, but the indispensable *first* thing, to do. Keeping the commandments is like peeling an orange. That's not the big thing either; consuming the fruit is. But there is no human way of enjoying the fruit without first taking the time to peel the orange.

The essence of purgation is *self-simplification.* Nothing can happen until this has proceeded a certain distance: until the involved interests and tangled motives of the self are simplified, the false complications of temporal life recognized and cast away. No one can be enlightened unless he be first cleansed, stripped, and purified.

Purgation for the sake of transformation of character consists of two essential acts: the stripping of that which is to be discarded; the cleansing of that which is to remain. One act is negative, involving as it does the repudiation of the superfluous, unreal, and harmful things that dissipate the precious energies of the self. This is the function of the virtue of poverty or the whole process of detachment, and may involve, for example, a repudiation of smoking, of excessive eating or drinking and a bad use of language, or the manipulation of a human person for one's own sexual pleasure or political advancement.

The other act is the positive one of raising to their highest term, their purest state, all that remains—the permanent elements of character. This is brought about by mortification, which deliberately embraces painful experiences and difficult tasks, such as an early rising time for some quiet time alone. Or it entails athletic and ascetic activities that prepare the whole man for God—for instance, a habit of discriminatingly good reading or a daily walk.

After being purged in the Mass we begin to be illumined by drinking in, digesting, and assimilating the Word of God through the liturgical readings. We climb behind the words and gaze on God. This is the illuminative way. We are now prepared to move into the crucial and decisive act of the Mass: the immolation. If the celebrants accentuate the banquet aspects of the Mass exclusively, then there is no sacrifice of the Mass and no eucharistic fruit to celebrate. If there is no immolation, there is no communion. What kills communion is the multiple intrusions of the ego. To live is to love, and to love is to suffer, to die, and to be reborn. The purpose of the Word is to *convince* us to die, to annihilate the superficial, empirical, separative ego; to get rid of the grasping, craving, dominating false self; to ready and steady us for the immolation.

We keep skirting the cross and the death and faking the resurrection, the festive celebration of risen men. We keep setting the table and inviting guests to the banquet, but on *this* side, the wrong side of death. We keep striving for communion without eliminating the obstacles to communion. We keep bludgeoning our way into I-Thou relationships with no authentic "I" to put on the line.

I am presently and poignantly witnessing a dramatic and tragic instance of this ego-fattening tendency to bypass the cross and indulge self-deceptively in a mock-merriment posture of resurrection. An artistic masterpiece, the finest and truest symbol of the Mystery of God and the Meaning of Christ I have ever seen, has been hanging over the high altar in the Holy Cross Chapel, Sedona, Arizona, for seventeen years. At the foot of this magnificent crucifix, sculpted by Keith Monroe, many lives have been radically changed. My own understanding of the historical, mystical, and cosmic Christ has been deepened immeasurably.

Cornelia Sussman describes this "Christ of the Atomic Age":

> Dominating the front view from the window, a great white cross stands in front of the altar. Nailed to the cross, a black, tormented Christ looks down through hollow eyes.
>
> One kneels. One crosses oneself. One dares not look up at this strange and terrible figure. One looks out through the enormous windows and thinks: The builders had no need for stained glass. God has stained the scene in this window with colors man can never reproduce. He has sculpted a scene beyond man's artistic feats.
>
> But it is not possible to distract the mind from the black figure of Christ, racked, stretched on the rack. One casts brief, hurried glances upwards. It is too cruel for contemplation.
>
> Have we done this to you, Lord? Is this what we have

done? Is this how you look after the concentration camps, the crematories, the salt mines, the torture chambers? Is this how you look after Hiroshima? Is this how you look after each atomic blast? Is this how you look after the fallout? Is this what we have done?

One turns away, observes one's hands clasped in prayer, but not before one has seen the feet, the black, swollen, unbeautiful feet.

Why do Your feet look like that? Have You been carrying this cross back and forth over a burning earth where no cool stream remained to ease those poor feet? Is that the atomic burn that nothing can ease, that burns and swells and blackens and still burns?

"What an atrocious cross!" a visitor, who had gone hastily outside, remarks. "Atrocious! It denies the resurrection of our Redeemer."

In his book *The Everlasting Man*, G. K. Chesterton says: "There is something appalling, something that makes the blood run cold, in the idea of having a statue of Christ in wrath. There is something insupportable even to the imagination in the idea of turning the corner of a street or coming out into the spaces of a market place, to meet the petrifying petrifaction of *that* figure as it turned upon a generation of vipers, or that face as it looked at the face of the hypocrite."

The figure of Christ which hangs in the Chapel of the Holy Cross in Sedona is not a statue of Christ in wrath; it is even more insupportable to the imagination, because it is a statue of Love physically ruined; and what is more insupportable than the image of *Love Embodied* tortured, burned, blackened and ravaged? Looking at this Christ . . . can one believe that *this* promises the resurrection, that Easter must follow, as inevitably as the day the night, this Good Friday? . . .

Here is the Christ of modern men, the Christ of the atomic age—blackened, ravaged, yet, like green-forested lava spilt round about, promising the new green life of resurrection.

Walking down the ramp of the Chapel of the Holy Cross, back to one's car, the thought that predominates is just that: a figure burned, tortured, blackened and ravaged, yet still promising the resurrection.

Can He still want us? Can He still love us?

It seems that He does. [*Desert Call: Special Anniversary Issue*, p. 19.]

Man cannot bear this much reality, this much love. The price of love is unbearable. Such a crucifix reminds us that even God suffers, and that we make him suffer in the atrocities of Indochina and the unrealities of Sedona. Comfortable, complacent men still find the real Christ to be scandal. Sweet innocuous images of the ugly, terrifying murder of Christ would be much nicer. Some rich people have convinced the bishop to take the atomic Christ down. So just as there are no blacks, no Indians, and no poor in Sedona, now there is no real image of Christ, the suffering servant. The "vipers" and the "hypocrites" are at peace.

If, in the Mass, we plunge into the death of Christ with such reckless abandon that we do in fact immolate the false self, then we will be drawn into holy communion with the Living God who will say: "Come to me all you who labor and are burdened, and I will refresh you. . . . I no longer call you servants but friends." This holy, active repose, this intimate spousal communion with God himself, symbolized effectively by the reception of the body and blood of Christ, is the *unitive way*.

What is also revealed in the Mass in a striking way is the marvelous balance between the ascetical and mystical dimensions of life. Obviously, there are positive and negative sides to the spiritual life, times to resist and times to yield, times to gain control and times to let go, a world to deny and a world to affirm. The man who pulls off the human adventure perfectly, who reconciles the yes and the no, the yin and the yang, the *ish* and the *esh*, is the *disciplined wild man*.

The surfer is my favorite example of the disciplined wild man, the man who has a perfectly balanced ascetical-mystical life. Check out his style. He gets up early in the morning. That's a tough ascetical act of self-denial. Then he attends carefully and reverently to his board, polishing and waxing it with love. Next he puts the board, this burden of love, this sacred tool, on his head and walks silently and solitary to the sea. There he faces a lonely and forbidding beach hardly perceptible in the fog. He then plunges into cold water, works his way out into the deeps against the waves, and now comes the keenest ascetical act of all: he waits; no impulsive action, no rush, no rash moves. He looks, listens, sees the distant waters, watching intently, contemplatively for the right wave, letting all the others go by. Finally, he sees the big wave coming. Deftly and adroitly he moves into position—timing is so important—not to master the wave, but to meet it and become one. They meet. He is caught up in the magnificent, mounting momentum of that majestic wave; his muscles relax, his spirits soar, he lets himself go, surrenders himself to the mighty swelling and roaring onslaught of that wave; and he rides and rides and rides in utter delight and sheer ecstasy. That is the mystical goal of a surfer's asceticism.

Such exquisite, abandoned delight in God's cascading glory, flowing through the parched human soil made ready for the pinnacle of all human achievements, spiritual matrimony with God, is the mystical goal of all man's asceticism.

CHRISTIAN EXPERIENCE

Chapter 9 – The Disciplined Wild Man

God is so infinitely lovable that once you get to know him you will have to love him, and once you love him, though you will enjoy a vibrant tranquillity of being, you will suffer an existential anxiety that his name be hallowed, his will be done, and his Kingdom come throughout the whole world.

Neurotic anxiety robs you of your creativity. But existential anxiety keeps you close to the vital center of the human adventure. It was toward that center that St. Paul went running, trying to sweep everyone into the race: "I am in anxiety until Christ be formed in you." Paul was racing toward the Christian goal: transformation into Christ. Transformation into Christ means *freedom*.

For the liberated Christian there is no law except *love*. As St. Bernard said: "To love God is to love him without measure." Such boundless love makes a man wild. That is why the Christian, or at least the saint, the really live Christian, must be a *disciplined wild man*. The conformation to Christ—thinking, loving, and acting like him—requires a rugged, unflinching discipline; but when the Spirit of God irrupts in man as he irrupted in Jesus, a christening transformation occurs, a fire is ignited; and for this man, blazing with the incandescent presence of God, no law is needed. The law has been fulfilled.

Even in all the updated religious constitutions I have seen there is a lingering weakness: the built-in assumption that the rule does not work. No one is asking the question "What do you do if the rule works?" No one wants to face that glorious possibility; because if the rule works, you have a liberated person, a saint, on your hands. How do you cope with that? You have in your midst an ordinary person who knows the secret of the universe, the mystery of God.

God's mysterious and momentous secret is not wrested from him by man's intellectual acumen or willful determination; nor is it stolen from him by the clandestine night raids of aggressive occultism or the Promethean pilfering of Pentecostalism. Neither is formidable self-control, flawless psychophysical development, or prolonged periods of meditative "sitting" necessarily the surest enticement or inevitable prelude to divine disclosures. According to the New Testament, it is only a man of contrite and humble heart whom God will not resist. It is up to God to reveal himself. It is obvious from the records of mankind that God has never revealed himself except to a man or a woman or a child of prayer. And a man of prayer is a man who lives by faith. Without faith there is no prayer, and without prayer there is no faith; at least, there is not enough faith to keep a man alive to God and open to the graceful possibilities of his own deification.

Faith is the response of the whole man to the Word of God ("I love you") and its reverberations in all creatures and all *human* events. Prayer is a spontaneous cry of the heart, sometimes in jubilant exultation, sometimes poignant anguish, often in the stunned silence of adoration or the transforming union of love.

Just as faith is a human response to the divine initiative, so prayer is a human response to the dialogic overtures of God. Prayer is the most personal act possible to man. Making prayer to God is more intimate than making love to a spouse. There is a part of a man so personally and privately inscrutable that even his wife may not trespass. This is equally true of the wife. This inner sanctuary of the human being is exposed only to God's holy scrutiny. It is precisely then, when man is most transparently exposed and radically embarrassed in the presence of God that he is most a man.

How can you plan on sharing that kind of prayer? Apart from the liturgy, it is hard to imagine shared prayer being a spontaneous cry of the heart at all. Prayer is often profaned and desecrated by rigid, static structures as well as by cozy, informal, "anything goes" shared prayer groups. Such groups often end up in therapy sessions and "heavy rap" sessions rather than prayer sessions. But since the conscious motive for getting together is prayer, the group ordinarily becomes unctiously and vociferously *prayer-conscious* instead of self-obliviously and worshipfully *God-conscious*. In place of prayer you get discourses, testimonies, emotional outbursts, and weird phenomena such as the "rift of tongues." You get the typical sensations of any "turned-on" group, but you get nothing like the Christian experience.

There is no evidence in the New Testament that Jesus ever got together with his friends for the express purpose of sharing prayer. He prayed in the Temple, of course, and he prayed on prayerful occasions when others happened to be around; but he was never involved in any prayer projects, programs, or groups. In fact, even when his disciples asked him to teach them to pray, Christ taught them the Our Father but did not pray with them. He did, undoubtedly, what the evangelists, especially Mark, said he was always doing: he went off by himself to pray. He practiced what he preached. What he preached is in Matthew 6:6: "When you pray go into your room, shut the door and pray to your Father in secret." The spirit of Christ, and therefore his prayer, was too wild to be corralled.

None of these remarks is meant to be a denigration of shared prayer. Various forms of communal prayer *might* be beneficial to certain people at elementary and uncertain stages of spiritual growth. But I am not sure that the minor benefits that just might accrue to a few justify the major risks imposed on all.

Prayer is such a free, spontaneous act of the person that it cannot even be taught. Some words that serve as vehicles of prayer may be taught, but not the veritable acts of prayer. Even in the Spiritual Life Institute desert house in Sedona, Arizona, or here at our hermitage in the woods of Nova Scotia, we do not attempt to teach contemplative prayer, even though our whole purpose is to live and share the contemplative life. All we can do is to set the stage as humanly as possible, immerse ourselves fully in life, and hope that God will sanctify us.

After all, God came into the world "that we might have life and have it more abundantly." He empowers us and challenges us to live fully and for this reason commands us to pray. Every decade the world will come up with reasons why we should or should not pray. It does not matter. Each one of us is commanded—not by the law, but by the Lord—"to watch and pray . . . to pray without ceasing." So even when there seems to be no reason to pray and no success at prayer, the faithful man prays out of obedience, and every time he prays, his life is enhanced and his world enlivened. A live man, perhaps devoid of any religious feeling but responsibly in touch with God through prayer, is one to be reckoned with. He alone can break through all the social, political, and religious barriers and become a transparent instrument of God's power and peace in the world.

What is required of all of us is that we venture forth as humanly as possible. The absence of prayer in the modern world as well as the bizarre forms of pseudoprayer is due to the dehumanized and denatured condition of man. We need to learn to be human again in order to pray. We need to become less crowded, less rushed, less dispersed, less victimized by the tyranny of diversion. We need to simplify our lives. We need to "collect" ourselves in periods of silence and places of solitude—not in order to withdraw or isolate ourselves from the others, but in order to relate more thoughtfully and lovingly to at least some of the others, if not all. *We need to learn to meditate.*

Prayer can best be appreciated once we have learned how natural a thing it is to meditate, how congenial it is to man, and how indispensable it is if he is to live a life that is fully human. Meditating liberates us from the compulsive drive of our desires; it evokes the deepest and most real dimensions of the authentic self; it *re-collects* the scattered forces of our fragmented lives so that we can discover the basic rhythm of human existence. In meditation, properly understood and perseveringly practiced, the whole man is actualized and the center of his being is awakened. The right thoughts, words, and deeds come to man on condition that he is awakened.

Meditation collects, unifies, and integrates a human being. Prayer raises the mind and heart to God. What's the use of coming into possession of myself, gaining mastery of my human instrument, if I cannot then put my beautiful "I" into relationship with the "Thou" of God? Why all this cold-blooded dutifulness if I cannot ultimately give my life away? Why prowl around in the fathomless and fuliginous abysses of my soul if I cannot find roots that become routes into a fuller life?

St. John Damascene's eighth-century definition of prayer as a raising of the mind and heart to God is a good one. From beginning to end the life of prayer is open-ended; and that is why the life of the man of prayer is characterized by wildness. The man of prayer is a man of God. God is wild. He is not a tame God. He does not fit into our world, our Church, or our plans. So the man of prayer, the mystic, passionately devoted to this untamable God, must be, though gentle and humble, an irrepressible wild man.

It is possible to talk about prayer in a hundred different ways. There are two dimensions I want to emphasize: "occupational" prayer and "spousal" prayer.

*

Occupation, according to the dictionary, is man's chief business, his vocation. A Christ-man, a man who responds to the sovereign claim of God with unconditional seriousness, certainly will not dissociate God from his chief business, his vocation. He will not relegate God and divine things to a separate compartment called religion. Since God holds the central place in his life and reveals himself to some degree in every other place, he lives all day in the presence of God. The divine presence is dynamic rather than static and so it flows into all of his thinking and all of his activity. His whole life is his spiritual life. But what gives quality and power to that pedestrian life of his is his *occupational prayer*.

Such a man knows that everything in this world is either a sign or a sample or a symbol of God. The universe is diaphanous.

The world is crammed with God. In every person or event met prayerfully, there is an overriding, transcendent, unconditional character that is captured in these words of the prophet, "Thus saith the Lord." In every situation this man of prayer is aware of being addressed, claimed, and sustained. And although this presence comes from *within*, there is something emphatically and *Wholly Other* about it. This immanent-transcendent convergence at the deep, prayerful level of a man's perception is the irreducible, ineffable mystery at the heart of all experience. "The beyond" is found in our midst.

Occupational prayer is possible, indeed inevitable, once man decides to live deliberately, because of the nature of man and God. "Man cannot rest until he rests in God." There is only one final love affair—the one with God—and our multilevel lives comprise one exploration into God. And as for God, his Being is in all beings. He penetrates the whole universe, so that every part of it exists in him, but his Being is more than, and is not exhausted by, the universe. So the author of *The Cloud of Unknowing* says: "He is the being of all. . . . He is thy being but thou art not his." So Teilhard de Chardin speaks of "that which in everything is above everything . . . shining forth from the depths of every event, every element," for those with eyes to see it. In Gerard Manley Hopkins's vivid words ("God's Grandeur"):

> The world is charged with the grandeur of God.
> It will flame out, like shining from shook foil;
> It gathers to a greatness, like the ooze of oil
> Crushed.

It is due to grace, to the diffusive nature of God in the world, that man is able to worship all day long at work and at play, in sickness and in health; man is in touch with the All—God, who is more real than he is, closer to him than he is to himself, the One who is ultimately and inescapably true. God makes love to us in wonderfully surprising ways. Worship is the response to him who, as Paul wrote to the Ephesians, is "above all and through all and in all." It is seeing all in God and God in all. Anything that discloses or penetrates through to this level of reality, whether in community or in solitude, whether in talk or action or silence, is prayer. In occupational prayer we discover God incognito: at one moment he is a cup of fresh water, the next a child bouncing on your knee, or a beautiful girl, or perhaps a morning walk or a nude swim in the moonlight.

I know a priest, a monk, who prays best sitting on the porch with his dog. He either talks to the dog about God or to God about the dog. And he gathers the whole world into that uplifting dialogue. I know a great big fat man who makes his best prayer floating in the ocean. With no one around to disturb him, the blue sky and brilliant sun above him, and the rollicking, rolling surf below him, he prays best. I know a college girl who makes her best prayer lying aimlessly on the beach, utterly drenched in the delicious sunshine of God's presence.

That was good prayer for the wee boy who came into church and right there at the door, sensing or intuiting God's holy, awesome presence, sank on his knees, bowed his head, and prayed: "O Lord, my name is mud." And in that brief moment of humble prayer and a posture of adoration (at least as effective, by the way, for contemplative centering as the lotus position) his soul was quieted and his being was deeply and divinely touched, and he felt in the marrow of his boyish bones and in the ebullience of his youthful heart the Sonship of Christ and the Fatherhood of God. There you have a mystic, one of God's wild ones. He has only to remain faithful.

I know a woman who makes her best prayer lying in the arms of her husband. Naked and exposed and vulnerable, she surrenders herself unequivocally to the Beloved through her spousal self-giving. Those who see sex simply as carnal knowledge will never realize the reverent and holy affirmation of Being, the deep and adoring worship, or the profound prayer possible in conjugal celebration.

*

God will never be the occupational center of our lives if we do not enjoy daily periods of *spousal prayer.* "Enjoy" is the right word, even though getting to prayer and staying there despite a dozen good reasons to do something else may often require a fierce determination of will. (Every time I swim I am thoroughly pleased and refreshed, but I often have to drag myself into the lake!) Enjoyment of God in daily spousal prayer is the doorway into the Kingdom, into the realization of divine union. "Knock and it shall be opened unto you." Knocking is the fierce and unflagging persistence of the lover who is always there.

According to a Persian love story, a lover came knocking on the door of the beloved. She said, "Who is it?" He answered, "It is I." She said, "Go away." He came back later, knocking even more urgently. "Who is it?" she asked. "It is I," said the lover. Again she said, "Go away." This time he went out into the desert, lived an ascetical life, and reduced his ego to zero. He returned, with a calm and relaxed certitude, to his beloved's house and knocked. "Who is it?" she asked. "It is thyself," he answered. And she said, "Come in."

We go to prayer because God is there. We want and need to be with him. If God is real and we are alive to him, then he must absorb us all by himself a good part of every day. If God is real, and we take him seriously, then he will draw us magnetically into prolonged periods of silence and solitude. Whether we have big jobs to do or children to feed does not matter. No other responsibilities compete with this one: to be with God, not indirectly and vicariously as we often are during occupational prayer, but directly and immediately, through intimate spousal confrontation. All the apostolic or prayerful work in the world cannot take the place of these intense and uninterrupted periods of leisurely lovemaking sessions between God and man. To work is not to pray. In fact, strictly speaking, these two terrific human activities are opposites. Work is the most useful human action, whereas prayer, at least at the highest levels, is the most useless. At those higher levels of prayer one would never think of using God; instead, all of one's energy is spent in loving, praising, and celebrating God, with no utilitarian designs at all.

The man who says he believes in God but is too busy to

spend any time alone with him in concentrated forms of prayer is like the man who claims he loves his wife but is too busy ever to be with her. He provides for her opulently, giving her all she could possibly need—house, car, clothes, swimming pool, pony—all, that is, except himself.

Without spousal prayer, occupational prayer is impossible; so is any worthwhile kind of apostolate, social, or political action, liturgical or family renewal, governmental or ecclesiastical reform, or a charismatic movement of any kind. There is simply no way for man to be humanized unless he is divinized by the spark of faith that is fanned into a blazing fire of love during silent and solitary periods of prayer.

Once the decision has been made to spend, let us say, an hour every day in holy leisure or spousal prayer, we need to experiment with all kinds of variations with regard to time and place until we discover the right time and the right place. Prayer will never be confined to then and there: it will simply be a favorite and most conducive time and place. One of the good results of the secular-ization process is the breakaway from an artificial and rigid dichot-omy between the sacred and the profane. We are now prepared to discover the sacred *in* the profane. But we still need the specially sacred places and the specially sacred times. This has been proven by all kinds of evidence. On the religious level, for instance, I have noticed with remarkable regularity how those houses that have abandoned specially sacred times and places for prayer, si-lence, and solitude have been, as an inevitable result, reduced to a shambles. Hugh Montefiore has made this point superbly:

> We need a symbol of the sacred in the midst of the secular to remind us that all is sacred and that we all have souls. The Church is a symbol of celebration and joy and leisure and privacy, a sign of transcendence and a point of silence and tranquillity; a church is sacred space, symbolizing to us the sacredness of all space.

I do not see how we can discern the revelation of God everywhere unless we find it, first of all, in the historical Christ and re-enacted in the Eucharist.

A favorite place for prayer may be on the roof, at the shore, on a mountaintop, in the woods, by the fireplace, in the bedroom, or in the chapel. But the best of all places for prayers will always be the Blessed Sacrament because it is a focalizing center where the personal embodied presence of Christ may be experienced with peculiar intensity. At our Nova Nada hermitage in Nova Scotia we have introduced all-night vigils in preparation for Sundays and feasts. It has not only heightened our prayer life immensely but deepened our view of the whole world.

Finding the right time is just as important as locating the right place. Variations in both time and place are helpful. But there will always be a particular time more conducive than others. Nighttime as high time for prayer is a possibility left unexplored by most people. We live such routine lives that even on a full-moon night the majority of us will be found in the same old condition in the same old place: sound asleep in bed. I do believe, however, that the best time of all is early in the morning. I would almost stake the possibility of a good prayer life on getting up early in the morning.

A somewhat prolonged period of uninterrupted time is imperative. Trying to squeeze God into a busy schedule does more harm than good. Whenever I emphasize prolonged periods of prayer, even to priests, ministers, and nuns, I am asked the same question, "How do you fit it all in?" The answer is "You don't." What we all must do is rearrange our lives so that we fit into God's plan; so that, first of all, there is time to relax in his presence. Prayer can be as refreshing as sleep. If we would learn to pray well, we could sleep less.

One final word on the subject of time: I suggest that we stop doing half the work that presently consumes us. Then let us attend to the remaining half wholeheartedly, with contemplative vision and creative love. I stake the authenticity of our lives and the effectiveness of our work on this radical shift.

*

Let us assume that a specially sacred time and place has been chosen for spousal prayer and a decision has been made to be there every day with unflinching regularity. What next? Preparation. The wise men and women of prayer tell us that preparation is the key. And they ordinarily designate two kinds of preparation; remote and proximate.

Remote preparation is, first of all, the way we think about God with our everyday minds. Prayer is primarily influenced by our general attitude toward God; and that attitude itself is shaped by our basic concepts and images of him. If we have poor concepts and puerile images of God, our prayer is necessarily impoverished. There is one attitude in particular that prevails today and spoils prayer; and that is our casual relationship to God. If God is just a three-letter word, or another being or just another object, then prayer will never erupt from the depths of our being. We cannot be casual with God and prayer. As Archbishop Anthony Bloom, Russian author of excellent books on prayer, says, every time we move into prayer we enter the cave of a tiger; and at that moment we are either condemned or saved. God is terrible and delightful. Only a dreadful experience of God readies us for a joyful one. We must be faithful and humble servants before we become intimate and ecstatic friends. We cannot bulldoze our way into his presence; we cannot even work our way meritoriously into his favor; we must be seduced. We do not choose God; he chooses us. "And this is charity, not as though we have first loved God, but that he has first loved us" (I John 3:10).

Here is a basic rule: *Be slow to pray;* be sure to pray but be slow to pray. God is not nice; he is not a buddy nor an uncle nor a mascot; he is an earthquake. We must approach him with fear and trembling. If we persevere in prayer without spiritual pride or greed, without skipping the humble steps of an obedient servant, we will end up enlightened and intimate friends of God. According to the Bible, the beginning of wisdom is fear. The fear Scripture refers to as the first step toward liberation is an ontological fear, a wonderful, awesome sense of the numinous, the Holy One. This is very different from the psychological fear that has turned so many religious men and women into either scrupulous, frightened neurotics or pious prigs.

We need to recapture the metaphysical awe of the pagans and the serious vigilance of the Jews. The encounter with God in prayer is like the momentous encounter with God in death. Here are the words of a great Jewish man of prayer, the Rabbi Schelomo of Karlin, one of the Hassidim of the eighteenth century. When he was asked to promise a friend a visit, he answered: "How can you ask such a promise? Tonight I will have to pray and when I pronounce the 'Hear O Israel' my soul steps out unto the very edge of life; then comes the darkness of sleep: and in the morning the great Morning Prayer that is a striding through the whole universe; and finally when I fall on my face, my soul bends over the edge of life. Maybe this one more time I will not die as yet, but how could I make any promise for after prayer?" Every time you pray you jeopardize your safety. It is a life-or-death situation. Without this attitude of *holy fear* there is no prayer.

The remote preparation is also the way we think of prayer. If we regard prayer as a duty, a mortification, or a chore, we will never pray well. If we identify prayer with meditation, our prayer life will be stunted and our laborious lives will not be relieved and refreshed the way they need to be. Meditation is the way we ready ourselves for prayer. When we really learn to pray, we seldom meditate. We need to meditate only when we are indisposed, out of touch with God.

If we think of prayer as nothing more than a means to an end, one of the ways by which we can manage to have a good day, we may be partially empowered but never wholesomely pleasured; and we end up using God, which is a deplorable thing to do. To pray in order to have a good day is not entirely wrong; as a secondary motivation it may even be good. A properly human perspective reverses this order of things: we see to it that we have a good day, by living deliberately and recollectedly, so that when it is time to pray, we are ready. Here we have a reversal of values based on the Gospels. The way we spend the day is the means; prayer is the end. We accept full responsibility for the quality of the day and look forward to the privileged periods of prayer when we can *do nothing*—because God is.

"The Father has uttered one Word: that Word is his Son, and he utters him forever in everlasting silence; and in silence the soul must hear that Word," spoke St. John of the Cross. This *wise passiveness*, not contrived by us or arbitrarily put on by us, but induced by God in us, turns out to be the most active and important part of a man's life; and without any fussing or fuming, man's consciousness is altered and his life radically changed. In other words, a life fully lived is the best remote preparation for prayer; and prayer is the best part of the day and the highest activity of man.

A peasant asked Giles, the Swiss hermit, what prayer was like. He said: "It's like going off to war or to a dance." Exactly! Prayer is a combat with God and for God. We will often be wounded like Jacob. But in the combat we will be, like Jacob, remade and renamed, if, like him "who wrestled with God," we refuse "to let him go." Prayer is also a dance with God; and that is why the man of prayer is always a tragic-merry man, a robust warrior who defends the rights of God and who dwells with God festively, serving him "wittily in the tangle of his mind," as Thomas More put it.

*

The *proximate preparation* for prayer is the particular way we choose to calm down and tune up immediately prior to the period of spousal prayer. This *centering down* ordinarily takes time, maybe fifteen minutes, which introduces another reason for a long, uninterrupted period of prayer. In the West the traditional way of achieving this serene and focused attention, a way proven to be eminently successful, is *meditative reading*.

In order to be effective, this kind of reading must serve the purposes of prayer. Books must be chosen with extremely discriminating taste and read meditatively. For instance, we cannot afford to read what is good for prayer, but only what is *best*. In a lifetime most of us will not find more than a handful of such books. The least helpful books are "meditation books." The most helpful are almost impossible to predict. The *Reed of God*, by

Carol Houselander, took me by surprise when I was a novice, and it kept me going all year and compensated handsomely for the dour dictates of the novice master and the lugubrious colloquies of St. Alphonsus Liguori. Some of the best books are not "religious" or "spiritual" at all, but have what it takes to shake off our lethargy, pierce our mental rigidities, and open us up to the transcendent dimension of life. *Mr. Blue,* by Myles Connolly, did this for me; so did *The Little Prince,* by Antoine de Saint-Exupéry; *Report to Greco,* by Nikos Kazantzakis; *Dr. Zhivago,* by Boris Pasternak; *The Chronicles of Narnia,* by C. S. Lewis; and some of the poetry of E. E. Cummings, T. S. Eliot, Gerard Manley Hopkins, and Rainer Maria Rilke.

Meditative reading is probably still the best proximate preparation for the typical Westerner but is, by no means, the only method. An exceptional film—*Rapture, Cool-Hand Luke, Women in Love, Man for All Seasons, Romeo and Juliet, Once upon a Time in the West*—or even a television program could do it, but certainly not as regular fare. Good music would be more likely; or perhaps a deep, quiet human encounter, a solitary walk, a bracing swim, or a romp in the autumn leaves or the winter snow. We tend to be so cerebral that oriental techniques—yoga, Zen, etc.— can be very helpful in *preparing* us for prayer.

There seems to be in the Western tradition a fairly consistent rhythm that unfolds, during a period, as well as throughout a lifetime of prayer. St. Teresa of Avila defines prayer as "a heart to heart conversation with God, our Father, who we know loves us." Why do we talk in our sleep? Because there is an image in the imagination so vivid it evokes a conversational response. So we begin with *imagination* in prayer. The world may be in a mess, it may seem like a gigantic dump, but the imagination is a good dump-picker. And with the help of an enlightened mind, it becomes progressively better. But the positively reliable storehouse for the imagination is the life of Christ with a thousand possible images. We need favorite images to pray by or, at least, to get started on our way toward prayer. St. Teresa's favorite image was

Christ being scourged at the pillar. Tessa's favorite image is Christ cooking fish for his apostles on the beach in the early morning hours.

The second noticeable feature of the ordinary pattern of prayer occurs when we begin to *reflect* on the Christ-image, or this biblical passage. This is *meditation;* and it should be obvious now that it is not identical with prayer but, rather, a step toward prayer. This involves far more than a private visit with Jesus. This is where and how we make our political and social as well as our religious judgments, decisions, and commitments in terms of the whole Christ. The whole purpose of imagination and reflection is to draw us into prayer—that is to say, into the *loving awareness of God.* This is prayer. Everything else is a preparation.

*

Growth in prayer is growth in simplicity. There will be less need for imaginative and meditative activities as the loving awareness becomes more intensive and extensive. We learn to pray the way we learned to read. At first we needed a constant supply of pictures. But if, in learning to read, we were never weaned away from the pictures, we would never have learned to cope with a page of words. In learning to pray, if God does not detach us from the baby food of the spiritual life, the images, pictures, and even concepts of God, we will never grow up into mature men and women of prayer, who cope no longer with graphic messengers and verbal ambassadors of God, but with God himself. Nothing but God, that is the heart of prayer. "And if you're lost enough to find yourself," writes Robert Frost in "Directive," "By now, pull in your ladder road behind you and put a sign up *closed* to all but me" (God).

To reach that utter simplicity, that pure human condition of *enlightened openness,* we must, with courage and alacrity, pass through the dark nights of senses and the spirit. These dark nights have been brilliantly outlined by St. John of the Cross in terms of a religious life. The mystic Doctor of the Church indicates how one may recognize the beginning of the Dark Night at which time God summons man into a deeper realm of faith. There are three signs:

(1) the inability to meditate—that is, to use reason and imagination in the things of God. God is communicating himself no longer by way of sense. He is transforming the strength of the senses to the spirit.

(2) There is no consolation from God, but neither is there from any creature. Imagination is restless. But there is no desire to fix the senses on the world.

(3) The mind is centered obscurely but lovingly on God. There is a certain deep-seated pleasure in being alone with God. There this loving, vague, general knowledge or quiet peace alternates with painful aridity and distraction, until it finally becomes habitual.

We must recognize the dark nights in the many secular forms they take these days as all kinds of people move from superficial levels of love and understanding into the depths. So many married people I know began to discuss divorce just when they were on the brink of a whole deeper dimension of love—love they never dreamed of—but they did not see the transitional nature of their dark night, with all its painful confusions and disabilities, which would lead them, bound faithfully together, into nuptial splendor.

So many religious quit the religious life just when they are ready to be led by the Spirit. They don't discern the positive features of the Dark Night and are frightened by the darkness, the wilderness, the desert, and they part with Christ in order to bask in the bright and shiny shallows of a mediocre Christian existence. College students leave the Church just when they are ready to move into dark but deep, pure dimensions of faith precisely because they cannot live on religious formulas, Christian doctrine, and articles of the creed. No one is there to tell them that this Dark Night is the entry into the real realm of faith, into a passionately personal relationship with the living God.

No wonder John of the Cross calls this desert experience a happy night, a "night more lovely than the dawn!" This night unites "the

Lover with His beloved, transforming the beloved in her Lover." It is the only way out of our present crisis of faith. All the livelier forms of faith and more fiery degrees of love and higher forms of prayer are on the other side of the Dark Night. The pattern of growth in prayer delineated by John of the Cross corresponds to the lovelife of the married couple, the vowed life of the religious, and the intellectual life of the college student.

What the mystics have called the *prayer of recollection* or *simple regard* is the result of a simplified and unified process of individuation; what has been called the *prayer of quiet* is due to the divinizing process whereby God asserts himself more manifestly into the consciousness of man and occupies the center of his energies. All higher forms of prayer are consequent upon the gradual deification of man who no longer follows paths paved by merely human industry, but follows an unpaved and untraveled road, led only by the Spirit into a realized union with God and a divine mode of existence. This is the goal of the human adventure.

There are Gospel principles but no blueprints for the human adventure. It is a unique and solitary journey. Life must be suffered in a total way that is totally new. It can be shared a little. But not death. Death must be taken alone. Once death is vanquished, and only then, can life be lived fully, exuberantly, divinely. The *All* that God promises is on the other side of death. The rules for attaining the All are joyful ways of dying.*

In the meantime, in the maelstrom, moving toward death with the same madness that impelled Jesus into Jerusalem and onto the cross, we live by flirting with death and embracing it—the way lovers do and wild men of prayer. The men of prayer are, in fact, the professional lovers of the world. Their vocation is to love. Where there is no love they put love, and then they find love. They know that they can "make nothing beautiful until they love it in all its ugliness" (G. K. Chesterton). That is why Christ's yoke is sweet and his burden light to them. That is why in the

* See John of the Cross's *Ascent of Mount Carmel*, Bk. One, Chap. 13, No. 11, New York: Doubleday Image Books, 1958; and Gertrude von le Fort's *Song of the Scaffold*, Kirkwood, Mo.: Cath. Authors Press, 1954.

throes of death, their laughter rings round the world and their prayer is always a spontaneous cry of the heart:

> Take me to you, imprison me, for I,
> Except you enthrall me, never shall be free,
> Nor ever chaste except you ravish me.
> —John Donne in *Holy Sonnets*, ll 12–14

Chapter 10 – The Failure of Christianity

If men in the Church are not driven by a transcendental hunger and thirst for God, then Christianity has failed.

If man, the restless pilgrim of the Absolute, the religious *hunter*, the nomadic wild man, does not pursue his prey passionately to the end, and does not find the real Christ, then Christianity has failed.

If man, once he has found Christ, does not recognize that the hunt is over, but the *human adventure* has hardly begun because now Christ, the active, hounding Lover, pursues man until he surrenders with reckless and total abandon to the sovereign claim of God, then Christianity has failed.

If men who profess "the faith" are not drawn and captivated forever by the infinitely attractive *existential Christ*, then Christianity has failed.

If even law-abiding men have lost their taste and capacity for God, then Christianity has failed.

If even morally upright men do not enjoy *the pleasure of God's company*—not a puny, sentimental enjoyment or lazy kind of delight, but the enjoyment of intellectual insight, loving awareness, personal encounter, challenge, discovery, exhaustion—then Christianity has failed.

If God is not real enough to absorb in the *art of contemplation* even the ecclesiastical leaders of the Church, then Christianity has failed.

If the schools, churches, and religious communities throughout the country are not at least half full of *earthy mystics*—people who know God by *experience*—then Christianity has failed.

If most of our college graduates are not *disciplined wild* men and women of prayer, then Christianity has failed.

If the present renewal going on in the Church does not lead the people way beyond the present preoccupation with threshold activities, ritual performances, and "churchiness," then Christianity has failed.

If the political, economic, industrial, scientific, and social pursuits of our nation are not being influenced by the spirit of the *existential Christ*, then Christianity has failed.

If love and freedom do not dominate a predominantly Christian community or nation, then Christianity has failed.

If Christians are not, as a rule, more human, more integrated personalities—*whole men*—because of their Christian spirit, then Christianity has failed.

If it becomes necessary for the state to solve the race problem in America, then Christianity has failed.

If the multiple Christian denominations cannot write and work together for the humanization of the world, then Christianity has failed.

If in the minds of the world leaders a continued stalemate is accepted, in practice, as "peace," and the power struggle continues under the constant menace of accidental global war, then Christianity has failed.

If proving the existence of God is still the central issue of religious teachers, then Christianity has failed.

If theologians are more concerned with the systematic theology of God than with the *God* of theology, then Christianity has failed.

If the bureaucratic or the organizational system of the Church swallows up or stifles the prophet and deadens the *heart of religion*, then Christianity has failed.

If the external management of the Church is so demanding that its shepherds become administrators instead of pastors, more concerned with public relations than mystical relations, then Christianity has failed.

Unless the Church's vital power and salvational import are manifested clearly and forcefully and *unofficially* outside of the religious ghetto in the secular sphere of the world, of the profane, then Christianity has failed.

Unless the dioceses and religious orders of the Church are not only spiritually renewed but structurally remade, then Christianity has failed.

Unless Christians become unhurried and unharried enough to enjoy *a long loving look at the real*, then Christianity has failed.

Unless Christians develop a conscience as free and creative as Socrates who said, "Men of Athens, I will obey God rather than you," then Christianity has failed.

The implication in each one of these instances, is, of course, that Christianity has indeed failed. It has not failed *finally*, in the sense that it is all over and the battle is lost: but it is failing its mission here and now.

There are ways out of this admission. There is G. K. Chesterton's way. He claimed that Christianity had not been embraced and found deficient: it had been found difficult and abandoned. But that is too easy a way out. And it is not entirely true. Father Vincent McNabb, that brilliant, colorful, and eccentric British Dominican, coped with it this way: Preaching in Hyde Park one day on the power, efficacy, and abundance of grace, a dirty, disreputable heckler asked, "If there's so much grace around, how come there aren't more saints?" Father Vincent McNabb could not resist answering, "Since there is so much water all over the world, how come you always have a dirty face?" And that is one answer to the problem of an ineffectual Christianity: people are just wading in it but not being inundated by it.

But it is not the whole story. The Church itself has failed. The powers of hell have not prevailed against it; but neither has the Church (its leaders, representatives, spokesmen) always heeded Christ's stern rebuke to Peter (already head of the Church); "Get behind me, Satan." Peter earned this rebuke because of a very subtle and respectable form of ecclesiastical materialism, which has always been the greatest obstacle to the mission of Christianity. A materialist is one who regards matter as primary and ultimate reality and spirit as secondary and incidental. I doubt if there are any theoretical materialists among the devout People of God. But in practice they abound: it is obvious whenever and wherever material goods are treated as more valuable than spiritual goods. Where the institutional factor plays an important part in a community, materialism is liable to prosper. The institutional factor does play a very important part in the Church, consequently materialism does tend to prevail.

The brick and mortar examples as well as displays of pomp and luxury are obvious. Less obvious, however, are the subtle forms of materialism we are all fairly guilty of; for instance, how many of us value external membership in the Church over union with God established by sanctifying grace? An even more subtle form of materialism is to prize the "possession" of grace without doing the human things necessary to become a *whole man*, vibrantly, exuberantly *alive* with grace. That parasitic, ecclesiastical materialism flourishes in the Church with peculiar vigor is no more a reason for discarding the Church than the fact that the green fly infests rosebushes is a reason for dispensing with roses. Without the institution, religion would degenerate into a mist of subjective feeling.

Materialism is, then, the main reason for the failure of Christianity. There are lots of extrinsic causes for which Christianity can bear no guilt. For instance, Christianity cannot be expected to transfigure those who reject it. Neither can it transfigure the abstract thinkers, the talkers, the armchair philosophers who *do* nothing—in other words, whose lives are no match for their thinking. Christianity has to do with human action. You cannot know or understand, says Christ, the Christian message unless you are willing *to do*. Christ is not insisting upon frenzied, fussy action, but quiet, deliberate action involving the whole man in the contemplation of God and the love of his world.

We can only blame the Church for its intrinsic reasons for failure. We are not talking about the failure or success of the Church with regard to the *jobs* it does, but only with regard to its central *mission.* The fact is that Christianity has done a superb job: the position of women has been enhanced; monogamy has become the rule; human love has been transfigured; slavery has been outlawed; liberty and equality have become ineradicable ideals; hunger and thirst for justice have gripped men's hearts; the religious myth of the political potentate has been shattered forever. Pope John created an ecumenical world; Pope Paul continues to guide the Church through this turbulent, zany age, resisting the extreme demands of both progressives and conservatives; in all of Latin America the Roman Catholic Church is becoming a major force for social and economic revolutionary change.

But here we are concerned solely with the single-hearted mission of the Church whose purpose is to be the prolongation of Christ in the world; to be the contemporary Christ; to exert Christ's own personal divine influence at the creative center of our culture.

If we are to ascertain the success or failure of Christianity, we must know exactly what the mission of Christ is. His mission is twofold: to show forth the Father and to unite us with the Godhead. In this way he satisfies man's twofold basic human need for intuition and for vital union. A man loves to see, admire, and contemplate good, beautiful things; he also loves to become in some way equated or identified with them. Thus you have always in the face of the true, the good, and the beautiful (wine, food, music, a woman, a man) the need for intuition and union. The mission of Christianity, therefore, is to enable man to see God and to be with God.

Christ is the supreme and most complete revelation of religious truth, of love, of the Godhead. He who sees Christ sees God; who enjoys him enjoys God; who does his will does the will of his Father. It is the mission of Christianity to keep the image of Christ alive and bright enough for men to see, to contemplate; and to keep the presence of Christ concrete, strong, and compelling enough for men to desire vital union. For this twofold mission Christianity—or the Church—needs a live theology throbbing with the inspired Word of God and glowing with his image, and a live liturgy full of the real, dynamic, irresistible presence of God. It is here, precisely, where Christianity has failed. It has, over the centuries, become so completely absorbed in jobs to be done, admittedly vastly important jobs, that it has neglected its mission.

God is so infinitely attractive that once you really notice him, you've got to love him. The trouble is that almost no one knows Christ, who is the revelation of the Father, the embodiment of God, the burning and glowing of God in our midst, God in his most appealing form. This is what Christianity is all about: getting to know Christ, becoming identified with Christ—thinking, loving, and acting like Christ.

Some years ago I conducted a survey among a few Catholic colleges trying to ascertain what the average Catholic college student thought of Christ. The results were disheartening. These students, for the most part, well versed in philosophy and theology, did not know Christ. Their education, insofar as it was specifically Catholic or Christian, was specifically a failure. After all, what does it mean to be a Christian? It means that Christ holds the central position in your life. It means that you are haunted and hounded day in and day out by his beauty, ever ancient, ever new. It means that you make all of your decisions and plans in terms of Christ.

Christianity has failed to convey to the world the real Christ. Without the vision of God there is no drive to become equated and identified with the Beloved, no vital union. You can increase and multiply and streamline all you want the liturgical participation of the people, but if this is not the embodiment of a genuine religious experience born of love through vision of God, then the people are engaged in empty ceremony, elaborate performances. Remember what Simone Weil said: "Of two men who do not have the experience of God, the man who denies him is perhaps the closer to him." I think she is right. (I am aware of the fact that the liturgy itself does convey the real Christ, but in practice the experiential discovery of Christ seldom occurs there.)

In the face of this failure all sorts of bad things have happened;

worst of all: men serve unreal gods and consequently live unreal lives, devoid of adventure. Voltaire was right: "If God created man in his own image, man has certainly paid him back in kind." We speak of God crudely, smugly, casually, obnoxiously as "the Man Upstairs." Because we go to church and receive the sacraments, we think we can speak as we please, as of someone whose every secret we know and whose every reaction we can guess. Most of the people in America who profess religion think of God in one of the following ways or a combination of them: a resident policeman preoccupied with ferreting out offenders; a meticulous bookkeeper who keeps strict account of our virtues and vices in his ledger; a fastidious schoolmaster always teaching us a lesson; a rigid customs officer whom we had better not try to deceive; or even one's own conscience—a conscience that grows largely out of convention and is usually overdeveloped or falsely trained or moribund. For others, God is like parents who have left a bad taste in our mouths because of their eccentricities and imperfections; or he is absolute perfection, and this sheer white cerebral abstraction induces us to have a nervous breakdown or become pious prigs.

Still others think of God as the Big Executive, and so they work out a cold, calculating relationship that is basically contractual: if we keep his commandents, then he must take care of us. If he isn't an executive, then he's an Elephantine Daddy, a concept that is largely responsible for so much religious thinking that is old-fashioned, irrelevant, and totally inadequate for today. It thus becomes impossible for religion to cope with the present real world. We are deluged with new knowledge and scientific advances, and we are trying to integrate them with obsolete concepts.

God in a box (in church) is a common religious concept that fragments man and turns the Lord into a cramped and regulated god who is a churchman. A variation of the same theme is "god in my head"—trying to fit the omnipotent, luminous, incomprehensible God of mystery and majesty into my cranium. The fact is that as long as we have neat, clean, tidy, categorical ideas of the divine person, then we are serving a false god. For more sophisticated believers, God is the providential law governing the universe unerringly. He is a distant god, aloof, indifferent to men's sufferings, who does not heed our prayers and lamentations, for the wheel of destiny is inexorable and blind, hurling innocent and guilty alike into oblivion.

Countless people still think of God as a limitless magician who can at random transform mice into men or carriages into pumpkins, or make statues weep and bleed; who can and does start and stop epidemics, repairs bones, and saves the life of the careless driver, scoffs at the laws of nature, and guarantees the eternal salvation of anyone who gets baptized, married, and buried in the Church. And highly educated missionaries still go, with animated and irrepressible zest, to the ends of the earth to save the "heathens" from the "jaws of hell."

Finally there is the *deus ex machina*, the makeshift god who is declared responsible for natural phenomena when scientists cannot discover their cause. These are just a few of the multitudinous distortions of God that dominate the religious attitudes of our Christian people. For a more elaborate list of pseudogods and an eloquent description of them, you may want to read *Our God Is Too Small*, by J. B. Phillips, though it was written quite a few years ago. We spend millions of dollars and utilize most of our manpower fortifying our Christian people against atheistic attacks from without and then let the people perish in a vacuum within— where there is no vision.

There are atheists whose intellectual probity and moral recti- tude bear witness to God, in that they have rejected the caricatures offered to them as true images of divinity. Certain forms of athe- ism are simply an indictment of infantile expressions of the faith. Atheists teach us not to cheat, and they reveal our subtle forms of idolatry. As Hans Urs Von Balthasar, the eminent contemporary theologian, points out: "The terrifying phenomenon of atheism might be, among other things, a dispensation of Providence de- signed to force mankind, and especially the Christian world, to return to a higher conception of God." Without an adequate conception of God there is no vision; with no vision there is no desire for divine union; without vital union with God there is no excuse for religion; and Christianity has failed.

But this is no reason for despair. Quite the contrary. It was the honest recognition of failure that inspired Pope John XXIII to call upon the whole Church to reform itself, and to set about it with the severity required for an examination of conscience. Pope John finally reversed the current: instead of congratulating himself upon representing the only true Church, he asked Christians to sweep their own doorstep and to turn their critical faculties in the first place upon themselves.

Despite the monumental harm done by absurd religiosity and ecclesiastical materialism, religion will not be destroyed. The Church is in touch with God, vibrant with his Spirit, rooted firmly and irrevocably in his Son. The Church is also in touch with the world, drawing its substance from all aspects of reality, not rejecting a single one. Sin itself has served as a springboard, ever since the cross was planted on Golgotha. Against this what could prevail?

The building of the Church will continue to the end of time. Twenty centuries from now, its appearance will be totally different, just as the Church today looks altogether different from the Church of the first centuries of our era. But behind all these changes of form, language, tradition, the same creative sap of freedom and love flows in from century to century.

Right now, in the middle of the twentieth century, we need hope. Hope is a supernatural force in us: our share in divine power. Hope is that virtue which reaches out infinitely beyond human reach into the Kingdom of God, striving for what is apparently impossible and insuperable. Hope emboldens us to undertake arduous tasks for God and for the world. It scorns ease and comfort and thrives on difficulties. It knows that if great trials are avoided, great deeds also remain undone, and in hugging to a miserable sense of security, the possibility of nobleness is utterly lost. We need to be challenged and provoked or else we become apathetic, unaspiring people. The human adventure is such a divine challenge that no man would dare undertake it without a divine *impetus* and God's promise of ultimate *fruition*.

A contemporary poet, Christopher Fry, was able to look out on the colossal chaos of our age, and, far from being discouraged, say:

> Dark and cold we may be, but this
> Is no Winter now. The frozen misery
> Of centuries breaks, cracks, begins to move;
> The thunder is the thunder of the floes
> The thaw, the flood, the upstart Spring.
> Thank God our time is now when wrong
> Comes up to face us everywhere,
> Never to leave us till we take
> The longest stride of soul men ever took.
> Affairs are now soul size,
> The enterprise
> Is exploration into God.
>
> —"A Sleep of Prisoners"

Bibliography

Baker, Augustine. *Holy Wisdom*. London: Burns & Oates, 1933.

Berger, Peter. *Rumor of Angels*. New York: Doubleday, 1967.

Bhagavad Gita. trans. Juan Mascaro. Baltimore: Penguin Books, 1962.

Bouyer, Louis. *Introduction to Spirituality*. New York: Desclee, 1961.

Butler, Dom Cuthbert. *Western Mysticism*. London: Arrow Books Ltd., 1960.

Chesterton, G. K. *The Everlasting Man*. New York: Apollo Editions, 1971.

The Collected Works of St. John of the Cross. trans. by Kieran Kavanaugh and Otilio Rodriguez with Introductions by Kieran Kavanaugh. Washington, D.C.: Institute of Carmelite Studies, 1973.

Donne, John. *Holy Sonnets*, no. XIV in Somer, John and Cozzo, Joseph, *Poetic Experience*. Glenview, Ill.: Scott, Foresman & Co., 1970.

Douglas, James. *Resistance and Contemplation*. New York: Doubleday, 1972.

Eliot, T. S. *Four Quartets*. New York: Harcourt, Brace & World, Inc. 1943.

Frost, Robert. "Directive," *Robert Frost's Poems*. New York: Washington Square Press, 1969.

Fry, Christopher. *A Sleep of Prisoners*. New York: Oxford University Press, 1951.

Hewes, Henry. *Best Plays 1961–62*. New York: Random Press, 1920.

Hopkins, Gerard Manley. *Poems and Prose* ed. by W. H. Gardner. Baltimore: Penguin Books, 1963.

Huxley, Aldous. *Grey Eminence*. New York: Harper & Row, 1941.

Johnston, William, S.J. *Christian Zen*. New York: Harper & Row, 1971.

Kerr, Walter. *Decline of Pleasure*. New York: Simon and Schuster, 1962.

Lewis, C. S. *Chronicles of Narnia*. New York: Collier Books, 1971.

———. *God in the Dock*. Grand Rapids, Mich.: Eerdmans, 1970.

———. *Letters to Malcolm: Chiefly on Prayer*. New York: Harcourt, Brace Jovanovich, Inc., 1963.

———. *Surprised by Joy*. New York: Harcourt, Brace & World, Inc., 1955.

Lynch, John W. *A Woman Wrapped in Silence*. New York: Macmillan, 1946.

Maeder, Michael. "Being Human—a Study of Friedrich von Hügel," *Sisters Today*, December, 1972.

Maritain, Jacques, *Reflections on America*. Staten Island, N.Y.: Gordian Press, 1973.

Mauriac, François. *The Stumbling Block*. New York: Philosophical Library, 1952.

Merton, Thomas. *The Asian Journal of Thomas Merton*, edited by Naomi Burton, et al. New York: New Directions Books, 1973.

Montefiore, Hugh. *To Help You Pray*. Naperville, Ill.: Allenson, 1958.

Moore, Sebastian. The *New Christian*, April 3, 1969.

Needleman, Jacob. *The New Religions*. New York: Doubleday, 1970.

Pfeiffer, Stephen. *Meister Eckhart—A Modern Translation*. New York: Harcourt, Brace and Company, 1958.

Ruysbroeck, John. *The Adornment of the Spiritual Marriage*. London: Dent, 1916.

Sussman, Cornelia. "Christ of the Atomic Age." *Desert Call. Special Anniversary Issue*, Sedona, Arizona; Spiritual Life Institute of America, May 1971.

Tamney, Joseph. "Religion as the Art of Suicide." *Listening*, Spring, 1968.

Tao Tê Ching. *Way of Life* trans. by Ch u Ta-Kao. New York: The Macmillan Co., 1959.